T0339185

Erased

Erased

VANISHING TRACES OF JEWISH GALICIA IN PRESENT-DAY UKRAINE

Omer Bartov

PRINCETON UNIVERSITY PRESS

PRINCETON AND OXFORD

Library of Congress Cataloging-in-Publication Data

Bartov, Omer.

Erased : vanishing traces of Jewish Galicia in present-day Ukraine / Omer Bartov.

p.   cm.

Includes index.

ISBN 978-0-691-13121-4 (alk. paper)

1. Jews—Ukraine—Galicia, Eastern—History—20th century.   2. Jews—Ukraine—
History—Galicia, Eastern—21st Century.   3. Holocaust, Jewish (1939–1945)—
Ukraine—Galicia, Eastern—Influence.   4. Galicia, Eastern (Ukraine)—Ethnic
relations.   I. Title.

DS135.U4B37   2007

305.892′404779—dc22

2007017231

British Library Cataloging-in-Publication Data is available

This book has been composed in Minion Typeface

Printed on acid-free paper. ∞

press.princeton.edu

Printed in the United States of America

1   3   5   7   9   10   8   6   4   2

In remembrance of

Ilona Karmel

(1925–2000), FRIEND, MENTOR, MODEL

I realize that your time in Cracow will be limited and that you both want and have to concentrate on the Jewish life there. But this is precisely my point: Jewish life, especially the life of the generation born around and shortly after World War I, took place not only, not even primarily in Kazimierz (the Jewish Quarter) but in the entire city. So that what Cracow represented became a part of us.
—From a letter by Ilona Karmel sent to me on June 2, 1997, shortly before my first trip to Eastern Europe

Ilona was born in Cracow and spent the war in the city's ghetto and in many labor and concentration camps. She subsequently came to the United States and published two outstanding novels based on her experiences during the Holocaust and her recovery from severe injuries at the end of the war: *Stephania* (1953), and *An Estate of Memory* (1969). She was an extraordinary woman and a great writer, and anyone who wishes to understand the term "crimes against humanity" should read her largely forgotten novels.

CONTENTS

INTRODUCTION

THIS LITTLE BOOK has deep biographical roots. It is also the first modest fruit of a long journey that began many years ago and has not yet ended. While it is not about its author, I cannot deny being more invested in it than in any of my previous historical writing. This is a story of discovery of what there once was, what has remained, and what has been swept away. This discovery was my own because when I began this journey I knew very little. Others who knew much more could no longer speak, or would not tell, or, most commonly, told only their own tales. I traveled into what was for me a white space on the map; there was a sense of adventure in this undertaking akin to what I felt when I read as a child about the great explorers of previous centuries. But it was also a journey into a black hole that had sucked in entire civilizations along with individual and never-to-be-met family members, making them vanish as if they had never existed, just as those explorers of old ended up transforming the white spaces on their maps into colonial hearts of darkness.

I spent much of my childhood and youth in a small neighborhood in northern Tel Aviv. Israel of the 1950s was poor, provincial, and isolated from the rest of the world. On a nearby hill stood the remnants of a Palestinian village whose inhabitants had fled during the fighting of 1948. It was populated by Jewish refugees from North Africa who had been expelled from their homes by Arabic regimes. My own neighborhood was soon inhabited by Jews expelled from Poland by the anti-Semitic postwar Gomułka regime, mostly survivors of the Holocaust and their children. Polish could be heard everywhere—at the grocers, the barbershop, the bank, and the post office. In my own home only Hebrew was spoken with the children. My father was born in Mandatory Palestine; my mother came from Poland as a child in 1935. But Yiddish was always an alternative, whether it provided expressions that Hebrew lacked or because it allowed grown-ups to speak about forbidden issues in front of their children. And because my mother's family came from Galicia, there was also Polish, Ukrainian, and some Russian, all blended together into a soft, foreign, but intimately familiar sound that still echoes in my head.

My generation, born in the 1950s, rejected this foreignness. We were socialized into a new Israeli society; our language was hard, direct, crisp Hebrew. We had no patience for the endless storytelling and punning of Yiddish, which seemed to us to be all about rhetoric and never about action, always observing reality by analogy and responding to events by recalling the past. As for Polish, it was the language of plump aunts with too much lipstick and rouge and of powerful vodka-drinking gentiles with Jewish blood on their hands. For us, enclosed in a narrow land surrounded by barbed wire and sea, the opening to the world was English: the language of pop music, long hair, and sexual liberation. It carried no echoes of ghettos, pogroms, and exile. Yet the sounds implanted in a child's mind rarely vanish; at some point in one's life they return, gently prodding, subtly directing the now middle-aged man to look back and listen to the inner voice of his past, to ask the questions that had never been posed: where, when, why, how?

I knew close to nothing about my mother's hometown. In fact, I knew very little about the world she came from, although I learned more and more about the manner in which it was destroyed. I spent many years studying modern German history, and especially that of the Third Reich. Thanks to my Israeli upbringing, I had internalized a great deal of knowledge about the Holocaust and at the same time rejected it as a subject of scholarly investigation: it was too close and traumatic to allow the necessary distance and had been manipulated politically too much to be salvaged from layers of empty rhetoric and demagogy. It was only in the late 1980s, when I came to the United States, that I felt liberated from these constraints to study the genocide of the Jews.

But I remained constantly disturbed by two aspects of the field that was quickly developing into Holocaust Studies. First, I felt that studying the manner in which the Jews were killed told one very little about the manner in which the Jews had lived; in fact, it brought them into history for the sole purpose of depicting their extermination. Second, it became increasingly clear to me that there was a vast gap between those works that reconstructed the planning and execution of the "final solution of the Jewish question" by the Nazi regime and its agents, and those that reconstructed the lives and deaths of the Jews in their towns, in the ghettos, and in the camps. It was as if the very same Nazi insistence on separating the perpetrators and their victims had also infected the historians writing about that period.

In 1996 I visited two seminars on the Holocaust in Germany. These classes were ably taught by distinguished scholars; the bibliographies were extensive, the many students attending were serious and studious, the presentations in class were well informed and well argued. But everything the students read and wrote had to do with the German perpetrators; not a single reading concerned the victims—not one testimony, one memoir, one historical reconstruction of Jewish life or death from a Jewish perspective. As I realize now, and did not then, there was also nothing about the world in which much of the killing took place, the social and political context of Eastern Europe. The Germans were studying how Germans exterminated Jews, even more tenaciously than Israelis were studying how Jews were murdered by Germans.

When I asked the students and their professors about this perception, they had a ready answer: the Nazis had dehumanized their victims to such an extent that they no longer existed for them as human beings. Hence, in order to explain genocide, one does not need to know anything about the reality of its victims, since it was of no importance to the killers. Others have since put this more sharply: German students want to understand German perpetrators; that is the essential question for them. It is an issue of empathy and legacy, of rage and frustration, both on the general and on the individual, intimate level. They ask, How could my nation have done this? They wonder, What did my grandfather do?

For me, this was an unsatisfactory response. Genocide, even one organized by a sophisticated bureaucratic state, is ultimately about some people killing other people. There is, I reasoned, always a point at which the killer encounters his victim; there is, even if only for a fraction of a second, eye contact, or at least some fleeting recognition of the other as a fellow human being, just as the victims cannot avoid recognizing the humanity of their killers, however inhuman their actions may be. Assigning the victims to the category of the "dehumanized," or assigning the perpetrators to the category of the "inhuman," is an easy way out. The horror and tragedy of genocide is that it is an event in which human beings, who under other circumstances could and sometimes did befriend or even love each other, are transformed into hunters and their prey. But how could one reconstruct that part of the story? How could one give back to both perpetrators and victims their humanity yet not deny or

obfuscate the atrocity? And how could one return the protagonists of the horror to their former existence as normal human
beings living conventional lives, and then bring them back to the
moment—often lasting weeks, months, even years—in which
they played their assigned roles in the genocide?

That same year I decided to interview my mother. There was
no particular link in my mind between the questions I had been
faced with and the decision to ask my mother to tell me about
her childhood in Galicia. She had left Europe four years before
the outbreak of World War II, and in that sense was not a
survivor. Apart from her parents and siblings who all came to
Palestine, and one uncle who went to South America that same
year, the rest of her family—which I had not yet quite assimilated into my perception of my own family—were murdered.
But her view was of the prewar, pre-Holocaust years, untainted
by any personal exposure to mass violence. And as she spoke, for
about ninety minutes, without pause, I realized that she had
never been asked about a childhood whose landscapes, sounds,
and smells had all vanished into an enforced oblivion, because
of commitment to a new land, an inability to return, a loss of all
that had been home and family, and a lack of interest by children
and friends. I also realized that my mother had had a happy
childhood in those regions that in my mind consisted mainly of
violence and hatred, fear and death. We made plans to visit her
hometown in what was by then independent Ukraine.

This plan was never realized. Two years later my mother
passed away. But by then I had conceived a way to approach
the bifurcated narratives of perpetrators and victims, to bring the
protagonists of the event together into one place, to which they
come as any other men and women would, and in which they
take up the roles dictated by the nature of the atrocity, even as
they perform these roles in accordance with their individual
traits, character, and upbringing. Little did I know that my

decision to focus on one little town in Eastern Galicia would take me on a journey into regions of intricate interethnic and interreligious relations stretching over several centuries, and further complicate any previous notion I had of a strict distinction between perpetrators, victims, and bystanders.

My initial thought was that by focusing on the events of the Holocaust in one town, I would be able to reconstruct the relations between Germans and Jews in much greater detail and to understand the extent to which they established some sort of human contact before the former murdered the latter. And, indeed, I discovered ample evidence that not only did much of the killing take place on the spot rather than in faraway extermination camps, but that before and even during a process of mass murder lasting many months, Germans and Jews often maintained a variety of relationships with each other, or rather, that in many cases more or less intimate relations and familiarity were followed by individual, one-on-one murder.[1]

I also discovered, however, that such relations did not occur in a social, political, or cultural vacuum. For the town of Buchach (Buczacz), which I most closely examined, and many others like it in Eastern Galicia, was made up of mixed populations of Jews, Poles, and Ukrainians, with the latter forming the vast majority of the rural population.[2] I was also increasingly

[1] See further in Omer Bartov, "Guilt and Accountability in the Postwar Courtroom: The Holocaust in Czortków and Buczacz, East Galicia, as Seen in West German Legal Discourse," in "Repairing the Past: Confronting the Legacies of Slavery, Genocide, and Caste," Yale University, October 27–29, 2005, http://www.yale.edu/glc/justice/bartov.pdf (accessed December 3, 2006).

[2] Throughout this text I transliterate the current Ukrainian rendering of place names after first providing some of the more common earlier non-Ukrainian designations in such languages as Polish, Russian, Yiddish, German, and where relevant, also other languages). This in itself is not an unproblematic choice, since most prewar residents of the towns I discuss knew them by

convinced that one would not be able to understand the manner in which events unfolded in these towns during the German occupation without tracing back the lives, cultures, coexistence, and conflicts of the different communities that populated this region for many centuries. I therefore decided to write a history, or, in fact, a sort of collective biography, of the town of Buchach, which would trace its existence from the very early beginnings in the fourteenth century to its demise as a multiethnic community during and in the wake of World War II. That book still remains to be written. The present book is in many ways an account of my initial plunge into the region and my encounter with a past mostly forgotten, a present committed to rewriting the past, and a kind of reverse archeological undertaking in which the last remains of destroyed civilizations are being buried under the new edifices of the new.

My journeys to the Western Ukrainian regions of the former Eastern Galicia had two main purposes. One was to work in the local archives, seeking documents on the lives of the different communities of Buchach and the relations between them over the centuries. The second was to see the town and travel in the region in order to familiarize myself with the landscape in which my protagonists had lived and the urban environments they had built for themselves. I was, of course, also going on the journey that had been planned with my mother. But by the time I went to Ukraine, my mother had been dead for five years. I went with two Ukrainian research assistants, Oleg Majewski and Sofia Grachova, both of Kyiv and originally from Luhans'k

---

their Polish or Jewish names and spelling. But because I am describing this region from the perspective of the present, I opted for contemporary designations, which, in any case, are unlikely to change from now on. I have, however, retained such conventional English names as Galicia (Halychyna, Galicja, Galizien) or Podolia (Podillia, Podole, Podol'e/Podoliia) for the sake of simplicity.

in Eastern Ukraine, and for part of the time also with our driver Zhenia from Ivano-Frankivs'k in Western Ukraine.

On one occasion, I was sitting in an archive in L'viv (Lwów, L'vov, Lemberg) with Oleg, he looking through Polish and Ukrainian documents, I through Hebrew and Yiddish ones. I had only told him a few days earlier that my family had come from Buchach. Oleg asked me, "Why are you not looking for your own family?" I responded that of course I would be glad to find such documents, but that this project was not about me and my family. As fate would have it, that very afternoon a slip of paper fell out of a folder I had been reading and landed on my lap. It was a confirmation that my grandfather's application for a certificate of immigration to Palestine had been approved, dated March 1935. The family landed at the port of Haifa in December that year. Had they waited another four years, I would not have been able to tell this story. My mother, uncles, and grandparents would have been lying in a mass grave in Buchach or turned into ashes at the Bełżec extermination camp. I could not, after all, detach myself from this story.

But this was not simply a journey of self-discovery. As I found that I could read Yiddish, struggled to learn Polish, made my way painfully through Ukrainian, the sounds of my childhood came back to me. As I traveled through time and space in Eastern Galicia, my grandfather's tales about forests and rivers, dwarves and giants, echoed in my memory. But what I was learning was much more important than that. I had to learn—often after already visiting them—the history of individual towns and communities, their moments of glory and demise, their accomplishments and their degradation. I had to imagine how—in the pretty little towns, the vast forests, the rolling hills—people who had lived side by side for generations were transformed into killers and quarry, how a few altruistic souls were drowned in an ocean of hate, greed, and incitement.

I had, finally, to rethink the very concept of what we have come to call the Holocaust, or genocide. Because in these little towns, in that corner of the world, this was no distant, neatly organized, bloodless bureaucratic undertaking, but a vast wave of brutal, intimate, and endlessly bloody massacres.[3] Far from meaningless violence, these were often quite meaningful actions, from which many profited politically and economically. And today, as independent Ukraine struggles to reassert its still intensely disputed national identity, this known, familiar, but deeply buried secret, emerges once more from the burial pits and ruins—not as an event to be remembered but as one to be cast away or rewritten in a manner that will serve the goals of those who have inherited the land.

[3] See further in Omer Bartov, "Les relations interethniques à Buczacz (Galicie orientale) durant la Shoah selon les témoignages d'après guerre," *Cultures d'Europe centrale*, 5: *La Destruction des confins*, ed. Delphine Bechtel and Xavier Galmiche (Paris: CIRCE, 2005), 47–67.

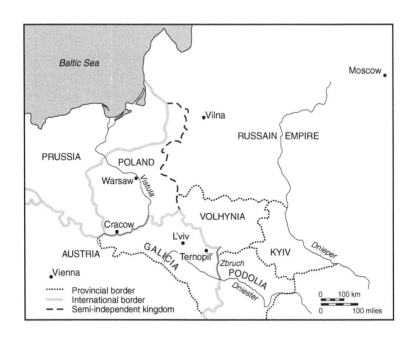

Map 1

Partitioned Poland and Galicia after 1815.

Map 2
The Districts of Eastern Galicia and Bukovina, 1910.

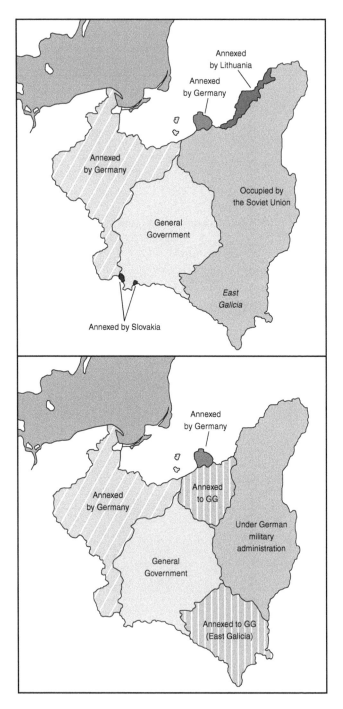

Map 3

Poland under Soviet and Nazi rule, 1939–1944.

Map 4

Oblasts and Raions of the former Eastern Galicia and Bukovina in
Soviet Ukraine, 1972.

Map 5
Independent interwar and postwar Poland.

Map 6
Independent Ukraine.

I

THE BORDERLAND

In 1772 the Habsburg Empire annexed the southern regions of Poland and created the province of Galicia. While Western Galicia was predominantly Polish, Eastern Galicia had a majority of Ukrainians. Following the collapse of the Habsburg Empire in World War I, Western Galicia became part of newly independent Poland in 1918. In Eastern Galicia, the Ukrainians established a short-lived "Western Ukrainian Republic." After more fighting between the Poles, the Ukrainians, and the Soviets, Poland annexed all of Eastern Galicia—made up of the provinces of Lwów (L'viv), Stanisławów (Stanyslaviv), and Tarnopol (Ternopil')—as well as the lands of Ukrainian-dominated Volhynia (Wolyń) and Belorussian-dominated Polesie (Western Belarus) to the north. These new borders were internationally recognized in 1923, and Eastern Galicia came to be known by the Poles as Eastern Little Poland (Małopolska Wschodnia). In 1939, as part of the Molotov-Ribbentrop Pact between the Soviet Union and Nazi Germany, Eastern Galicia—as well as the Western Ukrainian and Western Belorussian lands to its north—was annexed by the USSR and became part of the Soviet republic of Ukraine.

Following the German invasion of the Soviet Union in 1941, Eastern Galicia was annexed to the German-ruled General Government in Poland as Distrikt Galizien. In 1944 this region was reconquered by the Red Army and again became part of Soviet Ukraine. Since 1991 the former Eastern Galicia has been part of the western region of independent Ukraine. This borderland territory stretches from just north of the regional capital L'viv (Lwów, L'vov, Lemberg) almost all the way south to Chernivtsi

(Chernovtsy, Czernowitz, Cernăuţi) in the former Austrian province of Bukovina, and it extends from the Carpathian range in the west to the Zbruch (Zbrucz) River and the plains of Podolia in the East. It is a land that has many claims to fame and infamy.

Historically, Galicia constituted the borderland between the old Polish-Lithuanian Commonwealth—which was finally destroyed by the three partitions of Poland in the late eighteenth century—and the empires and marauders from the east and the south: the Tatars, the Cossacks, the Turkish Ottomans, and later, the Russians and the Soviets. It was a mixed bag of interdenominational and interethnic coexistence on the one hand, and of animosity, strife, and bloodshed on the other. Galicia was also the birthplace or breeding ground of many spiritual and political movements. Romantic Polish literature glorified the rule of Poland's great noble houses over these lands; Shabbateanism, Frankism, Hasidism, Haskalah (enlightenment) and, finally, Zionism flourished there among the Jews; Ukrainian literary and political nationalism found a firm base there and some of its most distinguished political and cultural figures came from the province's towns and villages.[1]

Galicia was a borderland in yet another sense: situated at the edge of East Central Europe, it was imbued with Polish, German, and Austrian cultural influences, but also open to the wide plains, forests, and steppe lands of western Russia and Asia, vast territories in which Europe was but a rumor. The Galician countryside was poor, muddy, backward, and primitive. Right across the border the author S. Ansky (1863–1920) launched his ethnographic expedition of the Pale of Settlement. Ansky sought the last remnants of medieval Jewish culture in the remote shtetlach (small and predominantly Jewish

---

[1] For the relevant literature see the section entitled "Additional Readings."

towns) of Russian Podolia hidden from the reach of modern civilization, and recorded his findings just before this entire crumbling world was swept away in the battles and massacres of World War I and all the horrors that came in its wake. It was in the Pale and in Galicia that Ansky organized relief operations for Jewish communities under a brutal Russian occupation during the war. And it was his familiarity with these regions that served as the background for Ansky's masterpiece, *The Dybbuk*, a mystical tale of soul possession and love set in a premodern East European Jewish universe akin to the one from which the author himself had fled decades earlier.[2]

Galicia was also where the peasants were imagined as the carriers of an authentic Ruthenian or Ukrainian culture and tradition, and where the splendor and heroism of the Polish *szlachta* (gentry) appeared to echo in the numerous castles built to ward off foreign enemies and rebellious serfs. Indeed, while the name Galicia no longer appears on modern maps and the names of its

[2] S. Ansky, *The Enemy at His Pleasure: A Journey Through the Jewish Pale of Settlement during World War I*, ed. and trans. Joachim Neugroschel (New York: Metropolitan Books, 2002), esp. xi–xiv. Originally published in Yiddish as An-Ski, *Der yidisher khurbn fun Poyln, Galitsye un Bukovine (fun tog-bikh TRED-TREZ—1914–1917)* (Wilno: Farlag An-Ski, 1921). Thanks to Delphine Bechtel for her help with this reference and other matters concerning Ansky. See further in David G. Roskies, introduction to S. Ansky, *The Dybbuk and Other Writings*, trans. Golda Werman (New York: Schocken Books, 1992), xi–xxxvi; Delphine Bechtel, "D'*Images d'un voyage en province* (1891) de Peretz à *La Destruction de la Galicie* (1917) d'Anski: Représentation des confins juifs entre expédition statistique et littérature," *Cultures d'Europe centrale*, 3: *Le voyage dans les confins*, ed. Delphine Bechtel and Xavier Galmiche (Paris: CIRCE, 2003), 57–76. Ansky was born Shloyme-Zanvl ben Aron Hacohen Rappoport in Vitebsk, a stronghold of Orthodox Judaism with a significant Hasidic presence. Vitebsk was also where Marc Chagall (1887–1985) was born a quarter of a century later, and it served as a model for the painter's depictions of what has become the stereotypical image of the shtetl.

towns and cities, as well as the identities of its rulers and inhabitants, have changed many a time, it remains the site or object of prejudice, legend, and myth, of nostalgia and regret, loss and oblivion. To be called "a Galitsyaner" (or Galitzianer) was for long not much of a compliment for its Jewish inhabitants: it denoted folksy backwardness and at times also a petty mercantile mentality and moral shiftiness. The Galitsyaner was someone who either spoke of leaving or had already left for better places (Vienna, Prague, Berlin, America—also known as the *goldene medine* [golden state] where money grew on trees and a Jew could make a living). Increasingly he or she came under the influence of Zionism and either dreamed of going to Eretz Israel or actually ended up in the Promised Land, discovering that it had very little to offer save for more hopes and dreams. But Galicia was also the land of great rabbis and yeshivot (religious colleges), of miraculous tales and vibrant community life, beautifully depicted in the writings of its great son, Yosef Shmuel Agnon (1888–1970), who recreated his hometown of Buchach as a microcosm of East European shtetl life, and given plastic expression in the paintings of Maurycy Gottlieb (1856–79) of nearby Drohobych (Drohobycz).[3]

---

[3] On the growing strength in the interwar period of modern Jewish national politics in Eastern Galicia, represented by the rival camps of Zionism and the anti-Zionist Bund (which sought to create a secular Jewish national life in Poland based on Yiddish culture), the waning fortunes of Agudes Yisroel (Agudat Israel) as the representative of Orthodox Jewry, and the crisis of Jewish-Polish politics in the 1930s, see Ezra Mendelsohn, *The Jews of East Central Europe between the World Wars* (Bloomington: Indiana University Press, 1983), 19, 50–51, 54–55, 68–83; Yisrael Gutman et al., eds., *The Jews of Poland between Two World Wars* (Hanover, N.H.: University Press of New England, 1989), 16–19, 24–25, 114–15, 123 (contributions by Ezra Mendelsohn, Gershon C. Bacon, and Antony Polonsky). For studies on the emergence of Polish nationalism and on Polish-Galician Jewish economy, emigration, and Zionism, as well as for memoir and travel literature on Galicia, see "Additional Readings."

Contemporary Germans, for their part, speak in terms of a rustic idyll about the former ethnic German population of Galicia, expressing a nostalgia documented in numerous recent books that must reflect disenchantment with the crowded modernity of the West and is all the easier to elaborate as the passage of time transforms memory into fantasy.[4] But German scholars have also recently reconstructed the destruction of the Jewish population in these regions.[5] For Austrians, a vaguely romantic view of their long-vanished great empire coincides with vicarious memories of what used to be its most backward province. Now a young Austrian historian has shown that this familiarity with the land and its people also facilitated the involvement of Viennese policemen in mass murder during World War II.[6] For Ukrainians, this western edge of their newly independent land—which, but for brief periods, had never been part of the Russian-controlled Territories of central and east Ukraine on either side of the Dnieper before the Soviet

---

See also the references there to the novels of the popular nationalist-romantic author Henryk Sienkiewicz (1846–1916); the works of the German-writing Jewish-Galician author Joseph Roth (1894–1939); Agnon's writings and biography; and Gottlieb's life and art.

[4] For studies of ethnic Germans in Galicia, Ukraine, and the USSR, see "Additional Readings".

[5] Dieter Pohl, *Nationalsozialistische Judenverfolgung in Ostgalizien 1941– 1944: Organisation und Durchführung eines staatlichen Massenverbrechens* (Munich: Oldenbourg, 1996); Thomas Sandkühler, *"Endlösung" in Galizien: der Judenmord in Ostpolen und die Rettungsinitiativen von Berthold Beitz, 1941–1944* (Bonn: Dietz, 1996).

[6] Thomas Geldmacher, "Die Beteiligung österreichischer Schutzpolizisten an der Judenvernichtung in den galizischen Städten Drohobycz und Boryslaw, 1941 bis 1944" (master's thesis, Vienna University, 2001); Geldmacher, *"Wir als Wiener waren ja bei der Bevölkerung beliebt." Österreichische Schutzpolizisten und die Judenvernichtung in Ostgalizien 1941–1944* (Vienna: Mandelbaum Verlag, 2002).

occupation of 1939–41 and after 1944—is both an example of greater western sophistication and a somewhat foreign and suspect region. Its Ruthenian farmers still till the black earth as their forefathers did, but as the different names of its cities and towns indicate, urban culture blends an assertive Ukrainian nationalism, traces of a rich Polish and Jewish past, and all the external trademarks of a spreading globalized modernity, even as many locals still refer to themselves as Galicians.[7] In all these respects, Galicia is a true borderland, the meeting place of numerous cultures, religions, and ethnicities, which is at the same time located at their periphery, a site where identity is all the more vehemently asserted precisely because of its often tenuous and fluid nature.[8]

Today's inhabitants of the former Eastern Galicia have little memory of its complex, rich, and tortuous past. This land is in the throes of creating a single national narrative of events, people, institutions, culture, and politics, an undertaking of massive simplification that not only distorts its past but threatens to impoverish its future. In a certain sense, this region exemplifies a larger trend that can be identified in much of the rest of Europe, claims to the contrary notwithstanding and despite differences in style and approach. The prewar world of Galicia is no more. But its past, and the denial of that past, is more

[7] "Forum: A City of Many Names: Lemberg/Lwów/L'viv/L'vov—Nationalizing in an Urban Context" (essays by Harald Binder, Anna Veronika Wendland, and Yaroslav Hrytsak), *Austrian History Yearbook* 34 (2003): 57–109; John Czaplicka, ed., "Lviv: A City in the Crossroads of Culture," special issue, *Harvard Ukrainian Studies* 24 (2000).

[8] For more on Galicia as a site of competing nationalisms, and the research project "Borderlands," see "Additional Readings." More generally on post-Soviet cities, see Elena Trubina, "Post-Soviet City: The Public, the Monuments, the Intellectuals," in *Lost in Space*, ed. Augustin Ioan (Bucharest: New Europe College, 2003), http://www.nec.ro/fundatia/nec/publications/lost.pdf (accessed December 3, 2006).

visible than in many other parts of Europe, thanks to neglect, indifference, and forgetfulness. Western Europe has rapidly modernized, and has thereby covered the traces of destruction with concrete and rhetoric.[9] Eastern Galicia was left on the margin, a borderland territory between the West and the East, with little development and investment under Soviet rule, and a seething nationalism that kept up resistance to the "liberators" of this land well into the 1950s.[10]

Since the early 1990s, the Soviet distortion of the past has been rapidly replaced by, or combined with, the previously suppressed nationalist narrative. But in many parts of the land these cosmetic changes have had little effect on the general condition of ignorance and abandonment, dilapidation and oblivion. Here the Galician past is still bare, indifference still glaring, prejudices and denials and fierce loyalties still almost entirely bereft of the comforting West European glaze of sophistication. The ghosts of the past still roam freely in the hills and valleys, clutter the unpaved streets, and congregate in synagogues transformed into garbage dumps and in cemeteries grazed by goats. And the inhabitants walk among the ruins and the ghosts, awakened to their presence only when asked by a stranger and forgetting them just as soon as he leaves. It is a region suspended in time, just for a little while longer, before it too will be swept with the tide of modernization and globalization, commemoration and apology. Sooner or later, the people of Western Ukraine's Galicia too will become aware of what they had lost and forgotten, but by then they will have destroyed these last material traces of the

[9] For the most recent example, see Karen E. Till, *The New Berlin: Memory, Politics, Place* (Minneapolis: University of Minnesota Press, 2005).

[10] John A. Armstrong, *Ukrainian Nationalism*, 2nd ed. (Littleton, Colo.: Ukrainian Academic Press, 1980), 290–321; Roger D. Petersen, *Resistance and Rebellion: Lessons from Eastern Europe* (New York: Cambridge University Press, 2001), 209–30.

past in their rush to catch up with the present and will have to recreate another past, one capable of more conveniently accommodating the spirit of tolerance and nostalgia that befits the modern temperament forged in the incinerators of difference and memory.

II

TRAVELS IN THE
BORDERLAND

FIGURE 1. The former Jewish quarter of L'viv in 2003 with prewar store signs in Polish and Yiddish.

L'viv / Lwów / L'vov / Lemberg / Leopolis

As WESTERN Ukraine's Eastern Galician territories begin to stir from decades of war, oppression, and economic decline, let us take a brief journey through this land of memory and oblivion, coexistence and erasure, high hopes and dashed illusions.[1] We begin in L'viv, now located some 40 miles southeast of the Polish border. Once a mostly Polish and Jewish city and a thriving cultural, economic, and political center, it is now struggling to emerge from the long years of Soviet neglect and suppressed memories of mass murder, expulsion, and demographic upheaval. Boasting a population of 830,000 people, the city is the capital of the L'viv Oblast' (region) and is the main urban center of what had been Eastern Galicia.[2]

Two sites may remind us of this city's past diversity. The Armenian Cathedral, dating back as far as 1363, is a well-preserved and moving edifice, testifying to the former presence of an important Armenian community in these parts of Ukraine (then Poland), most of whom eventually assimilated into the local population.[3] The Armenians—along with the Karaites and

---

[1] For accounts of other past and present journeys into these regions see "Additional Readings."

[2] Wikipedia, S.V. "Lviv," http://en.wikipedia.org/wiki/L%27viv (accessed December 3, 2006).

[3] One plaque on the building identifies it as "The Armenian Cathedral Church of the Assumption of the Virgin, 1363." Another plaque dates the

Greeks—were the main competitors with the Jews in com-
merce and business. Because they were Christian and therefore
assimilated more easily into the local population, and because
they numbered altogether far fewer people, the Armenian community declined while the Jewish population increased. Indeed,
just as Jews could maintain their identity in Christian countries, so, too, Christian Armenians retained a stronger sense of
their ethnic and cultural singularity in Muslim lands.[4] The Armenian Cathedral in L'viv is interesting not least because it
served as the burial ground for some distinguished Polish intellectual and political figures of the nineteenth and twentieth
centuries. This testifies both to the assimilation of the Armenians into the hegemonic culture of L'viv, and to the strong Polish
presence in a city that defined itself as an inherent part of
Poland despite growing pressures from Ruthenian/Ukrainian

---

building back only to 1578. A Ukrainian scholar dates the "Armenian Catholic
Church" to 1635. See Yaroslav Hrytsak, "Lviv: A Multicultural History
through the Centuries," in Czaplicka, "Lviv," 52. These different dates probably indicate reconstructions of the cathedral. Armenians have lived in East
Central Europe since the Byzantine era, dating back to the late sixth century.
The Armenian community in L'viv dates back to the thirteenth and fourteenth centuries. The community reached its height in the seventeenth century, when L'viv became the seat of an Armenian-rite archbishopric, and then
declined, numbering only three thousand by the early nineteenth century. By
this point the Armenian clergy and community were thoroughly Polonized.
See Paul Robert Magocsi, *Historical Atlas of East Central Europe* (Seattle: University of Washington Press, 1993), 110; Magocsi, *A History of Ukraine* (Seattle: University of Washington Press, 1996), 396. See also "Lviv," http://www.
armeniapedia.org/index.php?title=Lviv (accessed December 3, 2006); "Lviv
Tourist Catalogue-Guide," http://www.travel.inlviv.info/aguide/aguide5.php
(accessed December 3, 2006); Jeff Schlegal, "Heritage Survives a Compared
Past, Lviv, Ukraine," *New York Times*, July 23, 2006, http://www.nytimes.com/
(accessed December 3, 2006).

[4] Magocsi, *Historical Atlas*, 107–10.

nationalism and the predominance of Ukrainians in the surrounding countryside.[5]

The other site is the Golden Rose Synagogue, of which almost nothing remains. A modest plaque at the site carries the following inscription in Ukrainian, English, and Yiddish:

> Remnants of the old temple called "Di Goldene Royz." Built in 1580–1595 by the Nachmanowitch family in the memory of Rabbi Nachman's wife. The building designed by the Italian architect Pablo Romano, was destroyed by nazis [*sic*] and burnt in summer 1942.[6]

The site of the temple seems to be a popular nighttime hangout, as indicated by the empty beer bottles and other garbage strewn in the shallow pit next to the only remaining wall. The synagogue is located in the former Jewish quarter of L'viv, next to the old city wall. But one looks in vain for any explicit mention of the destruction of the Jewish community, let alone of Ukrainian collaboration. Nowhere is it mentioned that in the pogroms that followed immediately on the heels of the German army's entry into the city on June 30, 1941, somewhere between 7,000 and 10,000 Jews were murdered.[7]

---

[5] John Czaplicka, "Introduction: Lemberg, Leopolis, Lwów, Lvov: A City in the Crosscurrents of European Culture"; Hrytsak, "Lviv"; Alois Woldan, "The Imagery of Lviv in Ukrainian, Polish, and Austrian Literatures: From the Sixteenth Century to 1918," all in Czaplicka, "Lviv," 13–45, 47–73, and 75–93, respectively.

[6] This is the English text of the plaque. The Yiddish text is much abbreviated. The Ukrainian text is also slightly abbreviated, leaving out the fact that the synagogue was built to commemorate the rabbi's wife.

[7] Delphine Bechtel, "De Jedwabne à Zolotchiv: Pogromes locaux en Galicie, juin–juillet 1941," in *Cultures d'Europe Centrale*, 5: *La destruction des confins* (Paris: CIRCE, 2005), 69–92, esp. 72. For memoirs on the Holocaust in L'viv, see "Additional Readings". On Poles in wartime L'viv, see Grzegorz Hryciuk, *Polacy we Lwowie 1939–1944: Życie codzienne* (Warsaw: Książka i Wiedza,

Jews had already arrived in the region of L'viv in the tenth century, coming mainly from Byzantium and Khazaria, and the earliest Jewish tombstone found in the city dates back to 1348.[8] But the first signs of organized Jewish communities in western Poland don't appear until the eleventh, or more likely the twelfth century. Ashkenazi Jews along with other Central Europeans came to Poland during the following two centuries because of greater economic opportunities there. By 1500 the Jews of Poland numbered between 10,000 and 30,000 people and enjoyed the status of free men within the framework of a highly developed communal autonomy. On the eve of the Cossack-Ruthenian revolt of 1648 led by Bohdan Khmel'nyts'kyi (Bogdan Chmielnicki), Polish Jewry numbered some 450,000 people, and despite the devastation of the following decades the Jewish population grew to 750,000 by 1765. By then Jews constituted about 5.35 percent of the population of the Polish-Lithuanian Commonwealth. Created by the Union of Lublin in 1569, the Commonwealth brought vast areas of Ukraine—inhabited mainly by Ruthenians (later known as Ukrainians)—under Polish rule. Increasing pressure on Jewish settlement and economic rights in western Poland and offers of opportunities further east attracted many Jews to these new territories. By the mid-eighteenth century more than half of the Commonwealth's Jewish population lived mostly as town dwellers in privately owned latifundia under direct jurisdiction of the nobility; 44 percent of Polish Jewry lived in Ukraine-Ruthenia. Astonishingly, 80 percent of world Jewry

---

2000). For the history of Jewish L'viv, see N. M. Gelber, ed., *Encyclopedia of the Jewish Diaspora: Poland Series*, vol. 4, *Lwów* (Jerusalem: Encyclopedia of the Jewish Diaspora, 1956); Danuta Dąbrowska et al., eds., *Pinkas Hakehillot: Encyclopedia of Jewish Communities: Poland*, vol. 2, *Eastern Galicia* (Jerusalem: Yad Vashem, 1980, in Hebrew), 1–47 (henceforth cited as *Pinkas Hakehillot*).

[8] *Pinkas Hakehillot*, 1.

today can trace their roots to the eighteenth-century Polish-Lithuanian Commonwealth.[9]

The three partitions of 1772, 1793, and 1795 terminated the existence of Poland as an independent political entity until after World War I. As the Jews of the newly created province, or crownland, of Galicia found themselves under Austrian Habsburg rule, they lost much of their political and religious autonomy and underwent a progressive economic decline. Yet the Jewish population of Galicia grew rapidly from 250,000 in 1800 to 450,000 in 1857, despite significant emigration to Hungary. Three-quarters of this population was concentrated in Eastern Galicia, much of it in smaller towns and villages. In a poverty-stricken province, up to 80 percent of the Jews depended on the meager profits of trade for a living; especially among the poor, Hasidism became increasingly popular. That as late as 1910 some 60 percent of the Poles and 92 percent of the Ruthenians were engaged in agriculture exemplifies Galicia's backward economy. Indeed, by and large the gentile population was even poorer than the Jews, whose numbers reached 575,000 in 1869, just two years before the empire granted the Poles political dominance in the province. The following decades saw growing nationalism among all three main ethnic groups, with Jews responding to increasing anti-Semitism and grinding poverty by mass emigration: 85 percent of the 320,000 Jews who emigrated from Austria-Hungary to the United States between 1891 and 1914 came from Galicia. Many others moved to the larger cities

[9] M. J. Rosman, *The Lords' Jews: Magnate-Jewish Relations in the Polish-Lithuanian Commonwealth during the Eighteenth Century* (Cambridge, Mass.: Harvard Ukrainian Research Institute / Harvard Center of Jewish Studies, 1990), 36–41; Gershon David Hundert, *Jews in Poland-Lithuania in the Eighteenth Century: A Genealogy of Modernity* (Berkeley: University of California Press, 2004), 3–20. See also Martin Gilbert, *The Routledge Atlas of Jewish History*, 6th ed. (New York: Routledge, 2003), 32–33, 46–47, 56.

of Galicia or to Vienna. Those who remained behind were often politically mobilized by socialism, Zionism, and "autonomism," which sought Jewish political and cultural autonomy in the Diaspora.[10]

World War I devastated the province. As a consequence of brutalities and destruction by the invading Russian army, some 400,000 East Galician Jews fled to the west, even as others were deported to the east by the Russians. The subsequent fighting between Polish, Ukrainian, and Bolshevik armies was accompanied by such outbreaks of anti-Jewish violence as the pogrom of November 1918 in L'viv, when scores of Jews were murdered by Polish soldiers.[11] Under Polish rule in the interwar period the ratio of Jewish inhabitants within the total population of Eastern Galicia declined, and the Jews never recovered from the material and demographic damage of the war and its aftermath. Lack of economic prospects and discriminatory policies by the Polish government contributed to the growing popularity of political Zionism and the socialist Bund. By 1931 growing numbers of children were attending the sixty-five Hebrew language schools in Galicia.[12]

In 1931 East Galicia's 639,000 Jews made up 9.3 percent of the total population.[13] Most Jews lived in towns, but many of them actually resided in small shtetls (*shtetlach, shtetlekh*), and close to

[10] William O. McCagg Jr., *A History of Habsburg Jews, 1670–1918* (Bloomington: Indiana University Press, 1992), 109–22, 182–87. See also Alison Fleig Frank, *Oil Empire: Visions of Prosperity in Austrian Galicia* (Cambridge, Mass.: Harvard University Press, 2005), 24–47.

[11] William W. Hagen, "The Moral Economy of Popular Violence: The Pogrom in Lwów, November 1918," in *Antisemitism and Its Opponents in Modern Poland*, ed. Robert Blobaum (Ithaca, N.Y.: Cornell University Press, 2005), 124–47.

[12] *Pinkas Hakehillot*, xvii–xx.

[13] Pohl, *Judenverfolgung*, 43.

a quarter lived in villages. While the Jews increasingly identified with Polish culture, they found themselves caught between competing national claims by Poles and Ukrainians. Thus an urge to assimilate into Polish culture was accompanied by a growing attraction to Zionism, also fueled by postwar American restrictions on immigration and, especially in the last four years of the Polish republic, a surge in official and popular anti-Semitism. Ironically, during the interwar years Polish Jewry underwent a drastic transformation manifested in greatly accelerated acculturation, secularization, and modernization. This makes the fate of this community all the more tragic, as it found itself trapped between rival radical nationalists domestically and murderous totalitarian regimes across the borders, just as the gates of emigration either to the United States or to Palestine had virtually slammed shut.[14]

Walking the streets of the beautiful old part of town where the Golden Rose Synagogue is located, one still encounters the marks of mezuzahs on some of the doorways in Staroievreis'ka and Fedorov Streets.[15] Proceeding a short way further north

---

[14] Mendelsohn, *Jews of East Central Europe*, 18, 24, 40, 51–52, 82. In 1919–42 only 139,756 Polish Jews went to Palestine; this was a very high number for the Yishuv, the pre-state Jewish community in Mandatory Palestine, but a drop in the bucket as far as the three-million-strong Jewish population of Poland was concerned (ibid., 79). On the eve of World War II there were about 570,000 Jews in East Galicia. Following the German invasion of Poland they were joined by 130,000 refugees. In spring 1940 tens of thousands of Jews were deported into the interior of the Soviet Union. In August 1940 and May 1941 some 10,000 young men were called for service in the Red Army. Several thousand Jews escaped when the Germans invaded on June 22, 1941. There were about 620,000 Jews in East Galicia when it was occupied by the Germans in July (*Pinkas Hakehillot*, xxiii). Another estimate gives the numbers as 530,000 on September 1, 1939, and 570,000 on June 22, 1941 (Pohl, *Judenverfolgung*, 43–44). See also "Additional Readings."

[15] A Mezuzah is a parchment inscribed with religious texts and attached in a case to the doorposts of Jewish houses.

FIGURE 2. Doorway with mezuzah marking in L'viv, 2004.

from the center we reach the area of the oldest settlement of Jews in the so-called Cracow suburb, where the Great Synagogue of the Suburb (built in 1632) once stood. This was also a busy Jewish commercial district, and the peeling façades of the handsome nineteenth-century buildings reveal Polish and Yiddish store signs that were painted over after the original owners were murdered or expelled. One may assume that as the city modernizes, and its current inhabitants come into more money and renovate their houses, these last remaining traces of a vanished world will be erased. For now, very few people seem to notice them.

Nearby in Staryi Rynok (Old Market) stood the extraordinary edifice of the Reform Synagogue, also known as the Temple or the German-Israelite House of Prayer, of which nothing remains. It is now commemorated with a rough stone, about three feet high, to which a small plaque in Ukrainian and English is attached. The text reads: "This is the site of the Synagogue of the progressive Jews called the 'temple' which served Lvov's intelligentsia. It was built during 1844–1845 and was destroyed by German soldiers on entering to [*sic*] Lvov on July 1941."[16] The city has provided no other indication as to where the synagogue stood, and the site is therefore difficult to locate.[17] A couple of blocks away in St. Theodore Square still stands the former Hasidic Jakob (Yankl) Glazner Shul, built in 1842–44, which has housed the Sholem Aleichem Jewish Culture Society since 1991.

[16] Thanks to Delphine Bechtel and Sofia Grachova for pointing this monument out to me and to Artem Svyrydov for a photo.

[17] On tensions between Reform and Orthodox Jews in mid-nineteenth-century L'viv, see Michael Stanislawski, *A Murder in Lemberg: The Assassination of Rabbi Abraham Kohn* (Princeton: Princeton University Press, 2006). On the growing Polish orientation of the Jews of pre-1914 Lemberg as opposed to the persistence of German culture among the Jews of Chernivtsi, see Albert Lichtblau and Michael John, "Jewries in Galicia and Bukovina, in Lemberg and Czernowitz: Two Divergent Examples of Jewish Communities in the Far East of the Austro-Hungarian Monarchy," in *Jewries at the Frontier: Accommodation, Identity, Conflict*, ed. Sander L. Gilman and Milton Shain (Urbana: University of Illinois Press, 1999), 29–66, and at http://www.ibiblio.org/yiddish/Tshernovits/Lichtblau/lichtblau.html (accessed December 3, 2006).

Figure 3. The Jewish hospital in L'viv, 2003.

Most passersby presumably have little inkling of the significance of a plaque installed at the corner of the nearby Shpytal'na and Kotliars'ka Streets. Designed by the sculptor Pesach (Peter) Palit, who has meanwhile immigrated to Israel, the sign proclaims in Yiddish and Ukrainian: "In this house lived in 1906 the classical author of Yiddish literature Sholem Aleichem."[18] As its name indicates, Shpytal'na Street leads one to the vast Jewish hospital, built in striking oriental style at the turn of the previous century. While it cannot be mistaken for anything other than Jewish, since its tricolor tiled dome is decorated with Stars of David, no indication is given of its history. Behind the

---

[18] Tiqva Nathan, *The Last Jews of Lwów (Lemberg)* (Jerusalem: Reuven Mas, 1997, in Hebrew), 137.

FIGURE 4. The open market in L'viv, site of the old Jewish cemetery, 2003.

hospital was the old Jewish cemetery, first mentioned in archival documents in 1411 but known to have had tombstones dating back to the mid-fourteenth century. While its ancient stones were photographed before the war, the cemetery was destroyed by the Nazis, paved over by the Soviets, and now serves as the town's main open market, offering the kind of ragtag merchandise that clearly locates Ukraine on the periphery of Europe and in another historical time.[19]

[19] On the ongoing dispute over the Jewish cemetery in L'viv, see "Disputes continue around Jewish cemetery in Lviv," *Religious Information Service of Ukraine*, March 7, 2005, http://www.risu.org.ua/eng/news/article;4791/ (accessed December 3, 2006).

As we walk down another two blocks to Horodots'ka Street and turn into Hohol' (Gogol) Street, we find the former Jewish gymnasium, which now serves as Secondary School No. 52 without any indication of its former identity. Further on down Horodots'ka Street, as we turn into Brothers Mikhnovs'ki Street, we find the only functioning Jewish house of prayer in L'viv. Built in 1924 by the architect Aba Kornbluth, the Tsori Gilod Synagogue was meant to echo the tradition of the town's seventeenth-century Renaissance synagogues. By now, however, this small, dilapidated, walled-in structure, tucked away in a narrow street overlooked by the oversized neo-Gothic Church of St. Elizabeth, is one of the few pale echoes of the large and vibrant Jewish community whose 160,000 members constituted approximately 45 percent of the city's total population on the eve of the Holocaust.[20]

A good indication of the poverty of memory and the selective marginalization of the past is what one of the city's brochures calls its "biggest and interesting collection" of Judaica, to be found at the L'viv Museum of the History of Religions, housed in a former baroque Dominican Roman Catholic church and monastery near the Jewish quarter in the center of town.[21] The brochure assures tourists (if they can lay their hands on this hard-to-get pamphlet) that "this is the only museum in Ukraine, where you can see a permanent exposition of Judaism exhibiting approximately 100 original items." In fact, this collection, which will likely be moved out once the original

---

[20] Eliyahu Yones, *Smoke in the Sand: The Jews of Lwów during the War, 1939–1944* (Jerusalem: Yad Vashem, 2001, in Hebrew), 257. Also available in English: *Smoke in the Sand: The Jews of Lvov in the War Years, 1939–1944* (Jerusalem: Gefen, 2004).

[21] B. Mirkin, ed., *Jewish Heritage of Lviv*, trans. A. Turkivskyy (Lviv: Centre of Europe, 2002).

FIGURE 5. The Tsori Gilod Synagogue in L'viv, back view, 2003.

Roman Catholic proprietors reclaim the building from its current Greek Catholic owners, consists of a mélange of items that fill a couple of glass cases and have all the appearance of loot collected at the local flea market. Even compared to the far-from-impressive nearby exhibits of various Christian creeds, the Jewish "corner" looks like nothing more than a ghetto. The brochure informs us, however, that the "total number of [Jewish] articles rises to a thousand items in reserves of the museum. Primarily those are ritual articles of the seventeenth to the twentieth centuries." Remarkably, "among the ritual articles, torahs are the most valuable. The unique and biggest collection of torahs of the fifteenth to nineteenth centuries in

Ukraine (over 420 scrolls)," notes the brochure, "is located in the Museum of the History of Religions." Yet there is no access to these scrolls, and one must wonder about their condition in the basement of the church, and under what circumstances they might be allowed to see the light of day or be transferred to a safer resting place.

This brochure was kindly given me in March 2003 by Vita Susak, director of the European Art Collection at the L'viv Art Gallery, who noted that it was the last copy in her possession. Indeed, I have not been able to find the brochure anywhere else in the city. Ms. Susak also generously showed me around the gallery. While the permanent exhibition includes some fine works of Jewish artists and depictions of shtetl life in Galicia, the ultimate fate of the Jews is not mentioned anywhere in the gallery. In the somewhat awkwardly translated essay she contributed to the catalogue of the special exhibition, "Images of a Vanished World," mounted by the L'viv Art Gallery in 2003, Ms. Susak revealingly writes: "In my childhood, when reading ancient history, I was hardly able to realize how an entire people could have disappeared—Phoenicians, Copts, Assyrians and others. This is still unimaginable, although there was a tragic experience in the twentieth century, when there was an attempt to destroy the Jewish people. As a result, the Jews disappeared almost completely from the territory of Eastern Europe. People that were an integral part of the Galician cultural landscape, and gave a specific tint to the region, practically do not live any more on these lands. Today's little Jewish communities try to maintain existing monuments," she notes, "but every year this world has dissolved more and more into the past and has assumed the status of a myth." Hence, concludes Susak, the "main purpose of our exhibition has been to visualize this world on the basis of works of art," so as to form a "general picture of the Galician Jews life," which "allows the visitor to see

26

them as they had been before the homicide in the flames of the Holocaust."[22]

Several aspects of this essay stand out. First, it creates an association between ancient cultures that have long disappeared into the mists of the past and the destruction of Galician Jewry, which occurred within what is still the living memory of some survivors, bystanders, and perpetrators. Second, it speaks about this destruction either in passive or metaphorical language. Who it was that lit the "flames of the Holocaust" and helped stoke them or helped themselves to the property of those devoured by them is not mentioned: once upon a time there were Jews in Galicia, and now they are no more. Third, the process whereby the traces of Jewish civilization are vanishing is seen as quite natural, and no call is made to preserve any material remains, save for those still preserved in museums and art galleries. To this extent, my own melancholy reaction to the exhibition differed, I believe, from that of Ms. Susak. For I could not think of the lost world of Jewish Galicia as akin to the lost civilizations of antiquity, not least because I have personally known people who lived in Galicia. For her, I think, this was a vanished world whose past existence could only be experienced though artistic representations and museum artifacts.

[22] Vita Susak, "Images of a Vanished World," in *Images of a Vanished World: The Jews of Eastern Galicia (From the mid-19th century to the first third of the 20th century)*, Exhibition Catalogue, Lviv Art Gallery and the Dr. A. Schwartz International Holocaust Center, exhibition curators Halyna Hlembotska and Vita Susak, trans. Taras Kupriy, ed. Jeffrey Wills and Cristina Teresa O'Keefe (Lviv: "Centre of Europe" Publishing House, 2003), 6–12. See also Susak, "Les visages de la Galicie orientale dans les œuvres de ses peintres (fin XIXe – début XXe siècles)"; and compare with Delphine Bechtel, " 'Galizien, Galicja, Galitsye, Halytchyna': Le mythe de la Galicie, de la disparition à la résurrection (virtuelle)," both in *Culture d'Europe Centrale*, 4: *Le Mythe des confins* (Paris: CIRCE, Université Paris-Sorbonne, 2003), 189–205 and 56–77, respectively.

Since the fall of Communism, the destruction of the Jews of L'viv has received more attention. But it remains couched in euphemisms and distortions. In 1992 a Monument to the Lviv Ghetto Victims (1941–1943) was installed across from the railway bridge that had separated the ghetto from the rest of the city, as decreed by the German occupiers. Created by the sculptors Luisa Sternstein and Yuriy Schmukler, who have meanwhile immigrated to Israel, and the architect Volodymyr Plykhivs'kyi, this massive, quasi-abstract sculpture depicting an old Jew raising his arms to heaven in horror and supplication is surrounded by several inscribed stones, many of which refer to individual victims and must have been put there by members of their families.[23] Indeed, the monument itself was financed by the Jewish community of L'viv without any public assistance.[24] In front of the monument, under a steel menorah, is an inscription in Ukrainian that reads: "Remember and keep in your heart." A single memorial stone, lying flat on the ground, and inscribed only in somewhat ungrammatical English, provides an approximation of the events commemorated at the site: "Through this 'road of death' in 1941–1943 were passing 136,800 Jewish victims martyred by the German Nazi-Fascist occupiers in Lvov Geto [sic]."[25]

A second monument was erected next to the Yaniv (Janowska) concentration camp on the outskirts of L'viv in 1993 by Alexander Schwarz, a survivor of the camp who moved to Germany in

---

[23] Mirkin, *Jewish Heritage of Lviv*, 23; Nathan, *Last Jews*, 138.

[24] See Harold Marcuse, "Six Day Trip to Lviv, 5–11 August, 1999," http://www.history.ucsb.edu/projects/holocaust/LvovTrip/lvivjrnl.998.htm (accessed December 3, 2006).

[25] It is important to note, as I will mention below, that differences in the texts written in several languages indicate the real or anticipated sensibilities of potential readers as well as the agendas and historical understanding of those responsible for writing them.

FIGURE 6. The Monument to the L'viv Ghetto Victims, 2005 (photo credit: Artem Svyrydov).

1968. This was the site of the most murderous camp built in Ukraine, and one of the worst anywhere in Nazi-occupied Europe. Up to 200,000 people, mainly Jews, were tortured and killed there. After the war the Yaniv camp was used by the Soviet secret police for its own prisoners and later was employed for training police dogs and for breeding pigs. Thanks to Schwarz's pressure, this practice has recently been stopped, but his efforts to create a commemorative complex on the site of the former camp, which includes the killing grounds and the mass graves containing the remains of the victims, have thus far failed due to resistance from the local authorities. The entire area is still sealed off with a fence and cannot be entered. Only the memorial, which was erected in 1993 next to a locked gate, can be approached. This massive granite boulder carries the following inscription in Ukrainian, Yiddish, and English: "Let the memory of all the Nazi genocide victims in Janowska death camp remain forever: 1941–1943."[26] Reflecting his worries about the potential fate of such memorials in Western Ukraine, Schwarz has explained that he chose this boulder because "no one will have the insolence to blow up the ten-ton stone."[27] Nevertheless, while the number 200,000 and a Star of David are inscribed on the boulder, suggesting the magnitude of the crime and the identity of the victims, the word "Jew" is nowhere to be seen.

This is also the case with another memorial, or rather a large road sign, put up on November 19, 2003—the sixtieth anniversary of the camp's liquidation—next to the boulder and more visible from the road. Erected by the International Holocaust Center, a nongovernmental organization created by and named after Alexander Schwarz, the sign bears the following text in Ukrainian and (again, somewhat ungrammatical) English:

> Passer-By, Stop! Bow Your Head! There is a spot of the former Janovska concentration camp in front of you! Here the ground is suffering! Here the Nazis tormented, taunted executed innocent people and sent them to the gas chambers. Let the innocently undone victims be remembered forever! Eternal damnation on the executers.

[26] The Ukrainian and Yiddish versions are the same, save for using the word "fascist" instead of "Nazi," as was the convention in Soviet times.

[27] "The story of Lvov citizen Alexander Schwarz, who survived Janovska camp," http://www.history.ucsb.edu/projects/holocaust/Resources/Janow skaSurvivor047.htm (accessed December 3, 2006), site managed by Harold Marcuse, taken from Gundula Werger, "Denk ich an Lemberg," *Die Welt*, July 19, 2004.

This formulation further obfuscates the identity of the victims, never specifically identifying them as Jews nor providing any other symbolic indication of their identity. Ironically, the only hint that this sign has anything to do with the Shoah is its attribution, in much smaller letters, to the International Holocaust Center, which funded this commemorative plaque. This concealment of the identity of the very people in whose memory the sign was erected may have to do with the long-standing Soviet policy of never mentioning Jewish victims specifically; it may also reflect the fear of the small Jewish community of L'viv of stirring more anti-Semitism by insisting on Jewish victimhood. Either way, this text allows the local population to view the victims of the camp as "belonging" to them, rather than to a category of people whose history has been largely erased from public and collective memory and whose presence in the region has been almost entirely eliminated. The next generation may well grow up believing that the victims were simply Ukrainians.[28]

Similarly, the modest memorial located in the New Jewish Cemetery is visible only to those who enter this vast and crowded terrain of the dead, which is adjacent to the Yanivs'kyi

---

[28] See also "Seminars," http://www.holocaust.kiev.ua/eng/seminarse/lviv.htm (accessed December 3, 2006), the program of a conference that took place in L'viv in November 2003. Several Ukrainian institutions are listed as having participated, including the Regional Holocaust Study Center at the L'viv Polytechnic National University initiated by the Alexander Schwarz International Center "Holocaust" and supported by the Ukrainian Ministry of Education. The conference itself was supported by B'nai Brith "Leopolis: Association Leopolis, Humanitarian Assistance for the Ukraine," which also supports 10–15 percent of West Ukraine's estimated 12,000–15,000 mostly elderly Jewish population. Schwarz's association maintains a medical outpatient clinic and a pharmacy in L'viv, feeds 150 needy people in the cafeteria of the Polytechnic University, and provides food to the Jewish kindergarten. Alexander Schwarz was awarded the Order of Merit by former German President Johannes Rau.

(Janowski) Cemetery, on the road leading to the former camp, now renamed Shevchenko Street. Inscribed in Yiddish and Ukrainian, the memorial again avoids any mention of Jewish victims. The Yiddish inscription reads, "In eternal memory of the martyrs who fell at the hands of the cruel Hitler-murderers." The Ukrainian is even briefer: "In memory of those who perished in the years of Hitlerite occupation in 1942–1943."

It should be noted that most people in L'viv have no idea the Yaniv camp or its memorial exist. Even taxi drivers had to consult one another before identifying the site. This holds true for other Jewish sites in L'viv and in many other towns we will encounter later in this book. Such ignorance of the city's past is not only a feature of current educational policies or the Soviet ideological legacy, but also of the vast ethno-demographic changes in postwar Western Ukraine, especially significant in terms of the region's urbanization. Overall, Ukraine as a whole lost five to seven million persons in World War II, including some four million civilians. Proportionately, the Jewish population suffered most, but other ethnic groups also sustained severe losses due to death or migration. Consequently, ethnic minorities—such as Poles, Jews, Germans, and others—greatly diminished. If in 1933 Ukrainians constituted 66 percent of the population of Galicia and Volhynia, by 1959 they constituted 87.2 percent of the total population of Western Ukraine (consisting of Galicia, Volhynia, Bukovina, and Ruthenia), which numbered 7.8 million people, with the second largest ethic group at this point being Russians (5 percent).[29]

[29] The name Western Ukraine was given to the parts of Soviet Ukrainian SSR annexed between 1939 and 1945. They make up four historically distinct regions: Galicia (present oblasts of L'viv, Ivano-Frankivs'k, and Ternopil'), and Volhynia (oblasts of Volhynia and Rivne), which were under Polish rule until 1939; Bukovina (Chernivtsi oblast), which was under Romanian rule until 1940 and from 1941 to 1944; and Ruthenia (Transcarpathia), which was

In terms of changes in the ethno-demographic composition of urban populations the transformation has been especially drastic. Generally, in 1926 only about one in ten Ukrainians lived in cities or towns. In 1931 Ukrainians constituted only 16.2 percent of L'viv's population, whereas in 1970 they made up 76 percent of the city's inhabitants, the rest being mostly Russians.[30] Seen from this perspective, it is clear that the majority of Ukrainians in the cities and towns of the former East Galicia had not lived there during the war, nor had their ancestors, and they therefore had no direct memories or memories transmitted through the family of events there during the war and the Holocaust. It should be added, however, that Western Ukraine has resisted the process of assimilation into Russian/Soviet culture and language, and has insisted on its own distinct national character, more than any other part of Ukraine or other regions annexed by the Soviet Union after World War II, such as western Belarus (Belorussia).[31] In this sense, the lack of direct experience with the eradication of the large Jewish and Polish urban populations of the region may have made it even easier to recreate a historical narrative cleansed of the populations that had once been such an integral part of it.

Indeed, as L'viv has been reasserting its Ukrainian character, it has focused on depicting itself to the population as the main victim of totalitarianism, prejudice, and violence since time immemorial, and especially under Nazism and Communism. In this memory, there is no room for any other victims, let alone

---

ceded by Czechoslovakia in 1945. Roman Szporluk, *Russia, Ukraine, and the Breakup of the Soviet Union* (Stanford: Hoover Institution Press, 2000), 111, 139–40.

[30] Ibid., 141, 150.

[31] Ibid., 109–38.

for the victims of Ukrainians, and least of all, for the victims of Ukrainian nationalists, who can only be depicted as heroes and martyrs. L'viv has been undergoing a transformation whereby its streets have been largely renamed to reflect its Ukrainian character and a variety of monuments have gone up (this time financed by public funds) to celebrate its heroic Ukrainian sons.[32] But even in the monument to the victims of Soviet repression unveiled in 1997, which attempted to remind people that all nationalities had been victimized by the Soviets, the objective of reconciliation employed obfuscation and suppression of memory.

Erected in front of the old prison on Zamarstyniv's'ka Street by the sculptors P. Shtaer and R. Ryvens'kyi, the memorial includes the figure of a tortured, crucified man within the frame of a cross lined with barbed wire, surrounded by hundreds of names of NKVD (Soviet secret police) victims. The text on the monument reads:

> Between September 1939 and June 1941, within the prisons of Western Ukraine, 48,867 persons were killed. 1,238,256 were deported to Siberia. Within the prisons of the L'viv Oblast', during six days in 1941, 3,348 Ukrainian, Polish, and Jewish prisoners were shot.

Quite apart from the inflated figures, what this text obscures is the fact that the thousands of Jews brutalized and murdered by Ukrainians and Poles upon the entry of the Germans into L'viv were accused of being responsible for the murder of Ukrainian patriots in Soviet prisons. Precisely because it carries the three national symbols—the Ukrainian trident, the Polish eagle, and

---

[32] Yaroslav Hrytsak and Victor Susak, "Constructing a National City: The Case of L'viv," in *Composing Urban History and the Constitution of Civic Identities*, ed. John J. Czaplicka and Blair A. Ruble (Baltimore: Johns Hopkins University Press, 2003), 140–6.

the Star of David—thereby including the Jews in the general representation of victimhood, the monument liberates Ukrainian memory from the burden of invoking the mass crimes perpetrated by precisely those freedom fighters now celebrated as national heroes.[33]

This may be the right moment for a word about the alleged complicity of "the Jews" in Soviet repression during the occupation by the USSR of eastern Poland in 1939–41. Accusations of Jewish collaboration were common at the time among both the Poles and the Ukrainians. Indeed, if there was anything that these two ethnic groups agreed on—even as they increasingly engaged in mass violence against each other—it was their anti-Jewish sentiments, rooted in traditional prejudice and religious teachings, nationalist ideology demanding the cleansing of their societies of Jewish influence, and a view of Jews as either natural collaborators or synonymous with the Communists. For obvious reasons, the postwar Communist rulers of both Poland and Ukraine suppressed the view of the Jews as pro-Communist traitors of the nation, even as other anti-Semitic policies by these regimes were anything but absent. But with the fall of Communism and the reassertion of national sentiments, the old association between Jews and Communists returned, not least as a response to the growing evidence of collaboration in the Holocaust by precisely those nationalists who were now being lauded as the forerunners of these newly independent nations. But was there any truth to such obviously apologetic and self-serving allegations of Jewish collaboration?

[33] Bechtel, "Zolotchiv," 85; Liliana Hentosh and Bohdan Tscherkes, "Lviv: In Search of Identity—Transformations of the City's Public Space" (paper presented at Cities after the Fall: European Integration and Urban History Conference, Minda de Gunzburg Center for European Studies, Harvard University, spring 2005).

One point should be clear. When faced with the choice between the Nazis and the Soviets, Jews who knew about the anti-Semitic policies of the former obviously preferred the latter. Moreover, faced with the increasingly anti-Jewish policies of interwar Poland, not a few Jews, especially the young, believed that only Communism would assure just treatment for them in an era of growing radical nationalism and racism. The option of assimilation was largely barred by racist anti-Semitism, leaving Jewish nationalism, or Zionism, as the only alternative. But for vast numbers of Jews in these eastern lands, who were small artisans, shopkeepers, or merchants, Communism's only appeal was that it was less lethal vis-à-vis Jews than Nazism.[34]

Indeed, most Jews became quickly disenchanted with Soviet rule. Jewish political, religious, and cultural organizations were either entirely prohibited or greatly restricted; the teaching of Hebrew, which had become increasingly popular in the chain of Tarbut ("culture" in Hebrew) schools, was not allowed, and only Yiddish was recognized as the language of the "Jewish masses."[35] While more young men and women had access to secondary

[34] The best discussions of this issue are in Ben-Cion Pinchuk, *Shtetl Jews under Soviet Rule: Eastern Poland on the Eve of the Holocaust* (Cambridge, Mass.: Basil Blackwell, 1991); Dov Levin, *The Lesser of Two Evils: Eastern European Jewry Under Soviet Rule, 1939–1941*, trans. Naftali Greenwood (Philadelphia: Jewish Publication Society, 1995); and Jan T. Gross, *Revolution from Abroad: The Soviet Conquest of Poland's Western Ukraine and Western Belorussia*, 2nd ed. (Princeton: Princeton University Press, 2002), esp. "Historiographical Supplement: A Tangled Web," 241–88.

[35] In the fall of 1940 there were 1,003 Ukrainian-language schools, 314 Polish-language schools, 7 Russian-language schools, and only 20 Yiddish-language schools in the L'viv district, although Jews constituted 10–12 percent of the population there, not counting the thousands of refugees from German-occupied Poland. By January 1941 the number of Yiddish schools dropped to fourteen. Zionist Tarbut schools and Bund-sponsored Yiddish schools had all been closed by the Soviet authorities. Gross, *Revolution from Abroad*, 368 n. 66.

schools than had been the case under the restrictive quotas of the Polish regime, the new curriculum was based on a narrowly Marxist-ideological and Russian-nationalist worldview. Similarly, while some Jews were appointed to positions of power in the civil service and police, their numbers declined over time during those two years even as the presence of a mere handful of Jewish policemen on the streets might have seemed outrageous to Ukrainians and Poles precisely because it was unprecedented.

Conversely, the Soviets were hardly rejected outright by the Ukrainian population, which saw them both as liberators from oppressive Polish rule and as facilitators of a united Ukrainian state. Indeed, the Soviets introduced the teaching of Ukrainian on a large scale into schools and gave Ukrainians leading positions within the civil service. It was the Polish population that suffered most—and most immediately—from the Soviet occupation, as it lost its positions of power as well as its links to the Polish state. Poles were deported in large numbers by the Soviets into the interior of the USSR. Even so, proportionately, Jews were deported in even larger numbers than Poles, let alone Ukrainians, partly because many of them belonged to classes that were suspect from the Soviet perspective, and more importantly because a very high proportion of the numerous Jewish refugees from German-occupied Poland were soon thereafter sent further east by the NKVD. That the brutal deportations of about a third of a million people, rightly remembered by Poles and Ukrainians as a horrific and often deadly experience, actually improved the Jewish chances of survival was merely a function of the Nazis' determination to murder every Jew they could lay hands on.[36]

[36] Of 120,000 personal files of Polish citizens deported to the Soviet interior mostly in 1940–41, 52 percent belonged to ethnic Poles, 30 percent to Jews, and 18 percent to Ukrainians and Belarusians. The proportions of deportations stood in inverse relationship to the relative size of the main ethnic groups in these regions, where Jews constituted 10 percent, Poles were

The last wave of arrests and deportations by the Soviets, however, just before they were ousted from the former territories of eastern Poland by the invading Germans, was directed largely at Ukrainian nationalists. This meant that in the last days of the Soviet occupation the jails were filled with up to 50,000 people who were mostly, though not exclusively, Ukrainian. Of these prisoners up to 30,000 either were executed just before the Soviets retreated or died on forced marches to the rear.[37] This mass killing also meant that the memory and evidence of the atrocities was fresh on the minds of the Ukrainian population as the Soviets departed and the Germans marched in. The experience of suffering and slaughter, combined with the widely held view—strongly encouraged by the German occupiers—that the Jews were the true guilty party in Communist crimes, certainly played a major role in unleashing the widespread murderous

---

30 percent, and Ukrainians and Belorussians the vast majority of the population. The death rate among the deported was about 25–30 percent, very high, but far lower than the 90–95 percent death rate of the Jews who came under German occupation in these areas. If the Soviets had no "preferential treatment" for Jews, Communist Poland retained traditional anti-Jewish prejudices. Of 130,000 deported Polish citizens brought back to Poland from the USSR, only 8,000, or 6 percent, were Jews, although they constituted 30 percent of the total number of deportees (ibid., 269–70). Altogether from 1939 to 1941 between 309,000 and 327,000 people were deported from Western Ukraine and Western Belorussia; between 110,000 and 130,000 people were arrested (ibid., xiv, citing Stanisław Ciesielski et al., *Represje sowieckie wobec Polaków i obywateli polskich* (Warsaw: Ośrodek Karta, 2000), 11–16).

[37] Bogdan Musial, *"Konterrevolutionäre Elemente sind zu Erschießen." Die Brutalisierung des deutsch-sowjetischen Krieges im Sommer 1941* (Berlin: Propylän Verlag, 2000), 137–38. Musial's controversial thesis argues that the wave of pogroms following the Soviet withdrawal was triggered by the NKVD's murder of political prisoners associated with Jewish collaboration, which led in turn led to the brutalization of all involved, including the Germans, in the early phases of the Holocaust.

pogroms against Jewish populations in Eastern Galicia (and in other parts of eastern Poland). Thus, already at its second congress in Cracow in April 1941, the Organization of Ukrainian Nationalists (OUN) passed a resolution stating that "the Jews are the most faithful supporters of the ruling Bolshevik regime and the vanguard of Muscovite imperialism in Ukraine." It noted that the Soviet regime "exploits the anti-Jewish sentiments of the Ukrainian masses in order to divert their attention from the real perpetrators of their misfortune," and asserted that the OUN "combats the Jews as the prop" of the Soviet regime even as it "educates the masses to the fact that the principal enemy is Moscow."[38]

Even more disturbing, soon after his arrest by the Germans in July 1941, Yaroslav Stets'ko (1912–86), a leader of the OUN-B (the faction of the OUN headed by Stepan Bandera), wrote in his biographical sketch:

> I consider Marxism to be a product of the Jewish mind. . . . Moscow and Jewry are Ukraine's greatest enemies and bearers of corruptive Bolshevik international ideas. Although I consider Moscow . . . and not *Jewry*, to be the *main* and *decisive* enemy, I nonetheless fully appreciate the undeniably harmful and hostile role of the Jews, who are helping Moscow to enslave Ukraine. I therefore support the destruction of the Jews and the expedience of bringing German methods of exterminating Jewry to Ukraine, barring their assimilation and the like.[39]

---

[38] Taras Hunczak, "Ukrainian-Jewish Relations during the Soviet and Nazi Occupations," in *Ukraine during World War II: History and its Aftermath*, ed. Yury Boshyk (Edmonton: University of Alberta, 1986), 40.

[39] Karel Berkhoff and Marco Carynnyk, "The Organization of Ukrainian Nationalists and Its Attitude toward Germans and Jews: Iaroslav Stets'ko's 1941 Zhyttiepys," *Harvard Ukrainian Studies* 23, no. 3/4 (1999): 149, 170–71.

That the myth which propelled these massacres has been revived even in some recent historical debates, such as the one surrounding the mass killing of the Jews in the eastern Polish town of Jedwabne, indicates that this distortion of the past can also serve as a tool for inverting guilt and responsibility.[40] As a myth, the tale of Jewish collaboration with the Communists is as fascinating as the older and still potent canard of the *Protocols of the Elders of Zion*.[41] As history, it is simply false.

L'viv is the shop window of Western Ukraine. When one travels deeper into Galicia, one discovers even starker examples of Ukrainian self-glorification along with remarkable neglect, suppression, and even destruction of all signs of the land's multiethnic past and that past's tragic end in a campaign of mass murder and ethnic cleansing accomplished with a high degree of Ukrainian collaboration.[42] Let us then set out on our journey, circling

---

[40] The controversy was sparked by Jan T. Gross, *Neighbors: The Destruction of the Jewish Community in Jedwabne, Poland* (Princeton: Princeton University Press, 2001). Analysis and compilation of responses in Antony Polonsky and Joanna B. Michlic, eds., *The Neighbors Respond: The Controversy over the Jedwabne Massacre in Poland* (Princeton: Princeton University Press, 2004), 1–43. For depictions of "the Jews" as betrayers of the Polish nation and of anti-Semitic attacks as self-defense actions, see Tomasz Strzembosz, "Collaboration Passed Over in Silence," in Polonsky and Michlic, *Neighbors Respond*, 220–36; Marek Jan Chodakiewicz, *After the Holocaust: Polish-Jewish Conflict in the Wake of World War II* (New York: Columbia University Press, 2003), 131–48 (chapter entitled "Insurgent Self-Help or Polish Anti-Semitism?"). For the postwar Polish context of this argument, see Joanna Beata Michlic, *Poland's Threatening Other: The Image of the Jew from 1880 to the Present* (Lincoln: University of Nebraska Press, 2006), 196–229.

[41] Stephen Eric Bronner, *A Rumor about the Jews: Reflections on Antisemitism and the Protocols of the Learned Elders of Zion* (New York: St. Martin's Press, 2000).

[42] For literature on Polish-Jewish relations in World War II and before, see "Additional Readings."

the old province of Galicia in a counterclockwise direction, descending south along the eastern slopes of the Carpathian range toward the former border with Bukovina and then proceeding up north again along the Zbruch River and the old Russian border.

FIGURE 7. Cross over the Jewish cemetery in Sambir, 2006: "At this site are buried victims of Nazi and Communist Terror, 1939–1950" (photo credit: Oksana Sofiyantchuk).

Sambir / Sambor / Sambur

TRAVELING southwest from L'viv we come to the town of Sambir on the banks of the Dnister River. In 1939 the town numbered some 25,000 inhabitants, of whom about 8,000 were Jews. In his situation report of July 16, 1941, the chief of the Security Police and the SD (*Sicherheitsdienst*, or Security Service of the SS) in Berlin, Reinhard Heydrich, estimated that Sambir had a total of 26,000 inhabitants, among them 12,000 Poles, 10,000 Jews, and 4,000 Ukrainians. In early July 1941, as soon as the Germans entered the area, some 200 Jews were murdered in a Ukrainian pogrom, allegedly in retaliation for the murder of 400 Ukrainians by the retreating Soviets.[43] By July 1943, almost the entire Jewish population of the town had been murdered by the Germans and their collaborators either in the Bełżec extermination camp or in the town and its environs. In the latter years of the war and in its immediate aftermath the Polish population there too was either massacred by Ukrainian

---

[43] "Der Chef der Sicherheitspolizei und des SD, Berlin, den 16. Juli 1941: Ereignismeldung UdSSR. Nr. 24." Bundesarchiv Berlin (BAB) R58/214. Available also as "Operational Situation Report USSR No. 24: The Chief of the Security Police and the SD, Berlin, July 16, 1941," at http://www.einsatzgruppenarchives.com/osr24.html (accessed December 3, 2006); and at http://www.nizkor.org/ftp.cgi/orgs/german/ftp.py?orgs/german//einsatzgruppen/osr-ussr-24-c (accessed December 3, 2006). Presumably the number of Jews in town rose because of refugees from German-occupied Poland.

nationalists or forced to move to western Poland (previously eastern Germany).[44]

Contemporary Sambir reveals no traces of the composition of its prewar population or of the events that unfolded there in the second half of the 1940s. The town boasts several handsome churches, an elegant Habsburg-era gymnasium, a pretty town hall (*ratusha*), and a number of impressive townhouses. One of these houses carries a plaque put up in 1914 to commemorate the centennial of the birth of Ukrainian national poet Taras Shevchenko and proclaiming Sambir as "Ukrainian land." In the next building, a much more recent sign indicates the site of the Sambir branch of the "Social-Nationalist Party of Ukraine." The party's symbol combines an SS-like rune and a cross into a shape closely resembling a swastika, under which the words "the National Idea" are written. Transformed into a homogenous Ukrainian town, Sambir has shed much of its past and memory, save for the apparent predilection of some of its inhabitants for Nazi symbols and national-socialist "ideas."[45]

---

[44] Alexander Manor, ed., *The Book of Sambor and Stari Sambor: A Memorial to the Jewish Communities* (Tel Aviv: Association of Former Residents of Sambor/Stari Sambor and Their Region, 1980, in Hebrew and English); scanned copy, http://yizkor.nypl.org/index.php?id=2312 (accessed December 3, 2006); English translation, http://www.jewishgen.org/yizkor/sambor/Sambor.html (accessed December 3, 2006), esp. XXVIII, XLI; Pohl, *Judenverfolgung*, 64, 66, 224, 227, 240, 251–52, 255, 257; Sandkühler, *"Endlösung,"* 115, 349, 353, 360, 370, 374, 377; *Pinkas Hakehillot*, 345–46.

[45] The Ukrainian script appears as Iдeя Нацiї, rather than Iдeя Нацiї, using the Roman N for the word *Natsiï* (national) rather than the Cyrillic Н, presumably playing on the similarity between the Ukrainian word for nation, *natsiya*, and the term Nazi as the German abbreviation for National Socialist. For more on this party, look up its site: "kal'nyi ukrayins'kyi Natsionalizm," http://www.run.org.ua/ (accessed December 3, 2006). I would like to thank Marco Carynnyk for illuminating comments on the long tradition in Ukraine of replacing the Cyrillic Н with the roman N. This only seems to confirm my suspicion of a conscious allusion to Nazism in the case under discussion here.

FIGURE 8. Local branch of the Social-Nationalist Party of Ukraine in Sambir, 2004.

Since 1991, the town has also reconstructed its memory of the past by putting up a memorial to the victims of the NKVD in the yard of the district prison. The memorial, which includes a simple brick bell tower complete with a cross, carries two plaques. The first reads:

> In this district prison the Soviet punitive organs of the NKVD arrested over 5,000 people between the years 1939 and 1956. Hundreds of them, including Ukrainian gymnasium students, were shot and cruelly murdered. They were buried on the banks of the Dnister and Mlynivka Rivers, at the Jewish cemetery, and in the ravines by the city of Sambir. Eternal memory to them.

The second plaque reads:

> This memorial plaque was erected to commemorate the victims of communist terror, and as a warning to present and future generations.

The crimes against humanity perpetrated by the agents of the NKVD have no statute of limitations.[46]

Attempts to commemorate other aspects of the past, however, have been less successful. Thus the 2003 International Religious Freedom Report of the Bureau of Democracy, Human Rights and Labor, issued by United States Department of State, noted:

> In Sambir the Ukrainian Jewish community began construction of a memorial park at the site of an old Jewish cemetery and Holocaust massacre site with the assistance of a foreign benefactor.[47] Ukrainian nationalists, with the apparent assistance of local officials, erected crosses on the site to mark the Christian victims of Nazi terror there. While memorial organizers supported the recognition of all groups who suffered on the Sambir site, they opposed the use of Christian religious symbols on the territory of the Jewish cemetery. At the same time, local

[46] I would like to thank Sofia Grachova for supplying photographs of this memorial and translating the text on the plaques. It should be noted that for the Jewish cemetery the plaque uses the word *zhydivs'kyi*, still commonly used in Western Ukraine but considered pejorative in other parts of Ukraine and in Russia (as the equivalent of "kike" or "yid"), where the standard term for Jews is *yevreï*. There is some debate over whether the use of the term *zhydy* in the local Galician tradition actually carries an intentional pejorative meaning, is simply the correct terminology (related to the Polish *żydzi*), or reflects traditional and persisting local anti-Semitic attitudes. Some argue that for Ukrainian Galicians, *zhydy* is the standard, neutral term, whereas *yevreï* is pejorative because it evokes connotations to Soviet Jews and Russian/Soviet influence. However, during a debate over the return to old Jewish street names in L'viv that had been changed by the Soviets, it was decided not to use the original name of Starozhydivs'ka (Old Jewish) Street but to modify it to Staroievreis'ka Street so as "to avoid offending Jewish people," perhaps, it might be added, because many of the Jews in present-day L'viv came from Soviet Russia and would therefore be more sensitive to the term *zhydy*. See Hrytsak and Susak, "Constructing a National City," 156.

[47] This was an American Jewish descendant of Sambir.

FIGURE 9. Memorial to the victims of the NKVD in the yard of Sambir's district prison, 2004 (photo credit: Sofia Grachova).

Ukrainian nationalists remain opposed to the use of Jewish symbols or Hebrew in the memorial.[48]

It should be noted that the crosses in question in fact commemorate victims of Nazi *and* Soviet terror, whereas the Jewish community wanted to commemorate exclusively the Jewish

[48] See "Ukraine: International Religious Freedom Report 2003," http://www.state.gov/g/drl/rls/irf/2003/24441.htm (accessed December 3, 2006). Again, thanks to Sofia Grachova for drawing my attention to this event. See also "Country Reports on Human Rights Practices—2002: Released by the Bureau of Democracy, Human Rights, and Labor March 31, 2003," which notes that "in spite of a proposal by the memorial's foreign sponsor to relocate the crosses to another site at his expense, local government leaders still had not resolved the conflict by year's end." The report also notes that local

Figure 10. "To the victims of Communist Terror," Sambir, 2006 (photo credit: Oksana Sofiyantchuk).

victims of Nazi genocide murdered at that site. Indeed, it un-likely that the Soviets shot people on the grounds of the Jewish cemetery, and it remains unclear whether they buried there people they shot elsewhere. Either way, this is obviously an attempt to conflate Nazi and Soviet crimes and Jewish and Ukrainian victims by linking them all to the very same site.

While the United States Embassy has monitored this and other similar cases in Ukraine, and raised these issues with local and government officials, it appears that no progress has been made. In the spring of 2006, three crosses were still standing on the grounds of the Jewish cemetery. One large cross carried a plaque which read: "At this site are buried victims of Nazi and Communist Terror, 1939–1950. Eternal Memory to Them." The dates 1939–1950 are a clear indication of the urge to conflate Nazi genocide and Soviet crimes. A small, hardly visible plaque, obviously dating back to the Communist period, commemo-rated "the Soviet citizens" shot at the site by the Nazis. This was typical Communist practice: no mention was made of the fact that these "Soviet citizens" were murdered because they were Jews. At another site, away from the cemetery, one more memorial to the victims of the NKVD has meanwhile been erected, complete with a large cross and steel thorns, and inscribed with the words "To the victims of Communist Terror."[49]

---

officials in another town, "Volodymyr-Volynsky, Western Ukraine, continued to allow construction of an apartment building on the site of an old Jewish cemetery despite a December 17 court ruling to halt construction." http://www.state.gov/g/drl/rls/hrrpt/2002/18398.htm (accessed December 3, 2006).

[49] For photos of the cross at the Sambir Jewish cemetery and of another memorial to NKVD victims in Sambir, see "Poekhali: Ocheti o Poezdkakh v Razni Storoni" [Let's Go! Accounts of Journeys in Different Regions], http://mytravel.sbn.bz/base/view/gallery/1119267583 (accessed December 3, 2006). I would like to thank Sofia Grachova for alerting me to this site and for supplying high resolution photos of these edifices.

Drohobych / Drohobycz / Drogobych / Drohobets / Drohovitch

FIGURE 11. The "Choral" Synagogue in Drohobych in 1910 (photo of page in Roman Pastukh, *Vulytsiamy staroho Drohobycha*).

A SHORT DRIVE southteast of Sambir is the town of Drohobych, some 40 miles southwest of L'viv. Apart from the aforementioned painter Maurycy Gottlieb, Drohobych was also the birthplace of the great Polish-Jewish artist and writer Bruno Schulz (1892–1942). The famous Ukrainian poet Ivan Franko

(1856–1919) was born in a nearby village and attended school in Drohobych. Andrii Mel'nyk (1890–1964), the founder of the OUN, was also born in the vicinity. In 1939 the city numbered some 10,000 Poles, 10,000 Ukrainians, and 15,000 Jews. The German occupation began with a pogrom by local Ukrainians and Poles in which about 400 Jews were murdered. In the following three years the vast majority of the Jews were either deported to the Bełżec extermination camp or killed in the town and its vicinity. Most of the Poles were deported over the border to Poland.[50]

Those visiting Drohobych now would be hard put to discover any of its bloody history or the days in which it was described as "one and a half city: half-Ukrainian, half-Polish,

[50] For a history of Jewish Drohobych and its destruction, see N. M. Gelber, ed., *Memorial to the Jews of Drohobycz, Boryslaw, and Surroundings* (Tel Aviv: Association of Former Residents of Drohobycz, Boryslaw and Surroundings, 1959, in Hebrew and Yiddish); scanned copy, http://yizkor.nypl.org/index.php?id=2312 (accessed December 3, 2006); partial translation, http://www.jewishgen.org/Yizkor/Drohobycz/Drogobych.html (accessed December 3, 2006); *Pinkas Hakehillot*, 168–71. On the "Final Solution" there, see Pohl, *Judenverfolgung*, 70, 122, 143, 149, 190, 202, 224–27,243, 250, 256; Sandkühler, *"Endlösung,"* 303, 305–10, 312–18, 320, 323–29, 331–34, 336–39, 374–80, 398–99, 403. Further in Geldmacher, "Beteiligung"; and more generally, Geldmacher, *"Wiener."* In 1869 Drohobych numbered 16,880 inhabitants: 28.7% Ukrainian, 23.2% Polish or Roman Catholic, and 47.7% Jewish; in 1939 the respective figures for its 34,600 inhabitants were 26.3%, 33.2%, and 39.9%. By 1959, Ukrainians constituted 70% of the town's 42,000 inhabitants, Russians 22%, Poles 3%, and Jews 2%. In 2001 the population was 79,000 (estimated at 77,049 in 2005). Figures from Wikipedia, S. V. "Drohobych," http://en.wikipedia.org/wiki/Drohobych (accessed December 3, 2006) and *Encyclopedia of Ukraine*, S.V. "Drohobych," http://www.encyclopediaofukraine.com//pages%5CD%5CR%5CDrohobych.htm (accessed December 3, 2006). See also photos and text at "Drohobych," http://www.personal.ceu.hu/students/97/Roman_Zakharii/drohobych.htm (accessed December 3, 2006).

and half-Jewish."[51] As you park your car by the handsome park at the center of town, you glimpse a large statue at the point where all the paths meet. The oversized bronze figure of a man, standing with folded arms on a pedestal of Ukrainian granite, represents Stepan Bandera (1909–59), leader of the OUN-B, whose followers were deeply implicated in the genocide of the Jews and the ethnic cleansing of the Poles in Eastern Galicia.[52] The park, as it turns out, was built directly on the grounds of the ghetto into which the Germans crammed the Jewish population of Drohobych before murdering it. But there is no indication anywhere in the park that this was a site of suffering and slaughter by fellow citizens.

Across from the park, at the point where Taras Shevchenko Street merges into a shady boulevard (known before the war as the intersection of Czaski and Mickiewicz Streets), still stands the very same house next to which Bruno Schulz was shot by SS Scharführer Karl Günther on November 19, 1942, just as he was supposed to escape from the town. Günther had used the

[51] This saying is attributed to the Jewish-Polish writer Marian Hemar (pseudonym of Jan Maria Hescheles, born in L'viv in 1901, died in Britain in 1972). See Leonid Goldberg, "Drogobych—One and a Half City," *Jewish Ukraine* 7, no. 26 (April 2002), http://jewukr.org/observer/jo07_26/p0203_e.html (accessed December 3, 2006); Wikipedia, S. V. "Marian Hemar," http://en.wikipedia.org/wiki/Marian_Hemar (accessed December 3, 2006). See also Jaroslaw Anders, "The Prisoner of Myth," *New Republic Online*, November 25, 2005, review of Jerzy Ficowski, *Regions of the Great Heresy: Bruno Schulz: A Biographical Portrait*, trans. Theodosia Robertson (New York: W.W. Norton, 2003), http://www.tnr.com/doc.mhtml?i=20021125&s=anders112502&c=1 (accessed December 3, 2006); Denise V. Powers, "Fresco Fiasco," in *Forum: Żydzi-Polacy-Chrześcijanie*, May 6, 2003, http://www.znak.com.pl/forum/index-en.php?t=studia&id=67 (accessed December 3, 2006).

[52] Wilfried Jilge, "The Politics of the Second World War in Post-Communist Ukraine (1986/1991–2004/2005)," *Jahrbücher für Geschichte Osteuropas* 54 (2006): 50–81, esp. 55–56 and n. 30. See further in "Additional Readings."

FIGURE 12. Stepan Bandera's statue over the site of the former Drohobych ghetto, 2004.

opportunity of a "wild *Aktion*" by the Gestapo to avenge the killing of "his" Jew, the dentist Löw, by Schulz's protector, SS Hauptscharführer Felix Landau, for whom Schulz painted his last works.[53] In June 2004 I was walking with my Ukrainian assistants down the boulevard holding a book with photos of prewar Drohobych and trying to locate the site of the shooting when an old man approached us.[54] "What are you looking for?"

[53] Ficowski, *Regions*, 132–39. See further in "Additional Readings." The German *Aktion* (pl. *Aktionen*) and its Polish equivalent *akcja* (pl. *akcje*), as well as the Yiddish and Hebrew derivations (*aktsya*, pl. *aktsye* or *aktsyot*), denote roundup and mass killing.

[54] The book is Roman Pastukh, *Vulytsiamy staroho Drohobycha* (L'viv: Kamenyar, 1991); the photo is in a batch of plates between 64 and 65.

FIGURE 13. The site of Bruno Schulz's murder (prewar photo from Roman Pastukh, *Vulytsiamy staroho Drohobycha*).

he asked. We showed him the photo. "Oh, the spot where Bruno Schulz was shot," the man said, and led us to the house. He then motioned to the park. "This is where the ghetto was," he remarked. "I still remember it. I was a teenager at the time." Bandera's statue could be seen gleaming between the trees.

There is one spot in Drohobych where its illustrious son, rediscovered only decades after the war, is commemorated. A modest plaque is attached to the house where he lived with his family during the interwar period, at what was then 10 Floriańska Street. The plaque is recent; it may date back only to the controversy that surrounded the discovery of murals painted by Schulz in the room of SS-man Landau's son, large sections of which were removed shortly thereafter by agents of Yad Vashem in Jerusalem and taken to Israel.[55] "In this house,"

[55] Yad Vashem's agents had apparently struck a deal with the local Drohobych leaders behind the backs of the Ukrainian and Polish cultural authorities. On the controversy, see Ficowski, *Regions*, 165–72; Powers, "Fresco Fiasco"; Ruth Franklin, "Searching for Bruno Schulz," *New Yorker*,

FIGURE 14. The site of Bruno Schulz's murder, 2004.

announces the plaque in Ukrainian, Polish, and Hebrew, "in the years 1910–1941, lived and worked the famous Jewish artist and great writer in the Polish language, Bruno Schulz." This is a brave attempt to encompass in a single sentence the multifaceted nature of life, identity, and letters in those Eastern Galician towns before the catastrophe of World War II. It is a small, well-hidden attempt: the Schulz house is not even marked on the city map. Nor can one find the "villa" in which Schulz painted

---

December 16, 2002, http://www.newyorker.com/critics/books/?021216crbo_books (accessed December 3, 2006); Anne Applebaum, "An Oddball Miles from Anywhere," *Spectator*, March 15, 2003: http://www.anneapplebaum.com/other/2003/03_15_spec_oddball.html (accessed December 3, 2006).

the murals discovered there in 2001 by the German documentary filmmaker Benjamin Geissler, whose removal from the wall and transportation to Israel by agents of Yad Vashem was greeted with vehement criticism by Ukrainians and Poles alike. Suddenly everyone wanted to appropriate Schulz, who was shot like a stray dog on a nearby street six decades earlier.[56] Not far from the Schulz house is the gymnasium, where Bruno studied between 1902 and 1910 and where he taught between 1924 and 1939. We continue to Lesi Ukrayinky Street, where we find the former Jewish orphanage. Not many changes have been made to this handsome building. But the crescent-shaped sign above the main entrance, bearing the designation "Jewish Orphanage" in Polish, has been rather amateurishly erased, and the original Star of David design of the two round windows on either side of the sign has been altered.[57] We then reach Mazepa Street, formerly known as Sholem Aleichem

[56] Obviously damaging the mural and carting it off was hardly a satisfactory manner of dealing with this find, and the fact that the sections of the mural taken off to Israel have not since been exhibited at Yad Vashem is just as troubling. Conversely, judging by the state of other remnants of Jewish life in Western Ukraine, one would be justified in expressing skepticism about the willingness of the local municipality to preserve and exhibit the murals. Polish claims that Schulz "belongs" to their cultural heritage are as problematic as those of the Israelis: the heritage he actually belonged to has no obvious successors since the world in which he lived and worked was completely eradicated and erased; in Drohobych, as elsewhere, Ukrainians and Poles played an as yet unacknowledged role in this very process of eradication. See also Amiran Barkat, "Yad Vashem Not Displaying Bruno Schulz Holocaust Art," *Haaretz*, July 4, 2005, http://www.isjm.org/news/040805har.htm (accessed December 3, 2006); Benjamin Paloff, "Who Owns Bruno Schulz? Poland Stumbles over Its Jewish Past," *Boston Review*, December 2004/January 2005, http://bostonreview.net/BR29.6/paloff.html (accessed December 3, 2006).

[57] A photo of the building before the war can be found in Pastukh, *Vulytsi-amy*, between 64 and 65. It is not clear whether these changes were made under Soviet rule or since Ukrainian independence.

FIGURE 15. Drohobych city synagogue in 1909 (from Roman Pastukh, *Vulytsiamy staroho Drohobycha*).

Street after the great Yiddish writer who was born in Pereyaslav, near Kyiv, in 1859, and died in New York City in 1916. Schulz had known it as Stryjska Street, and it featured as such in his fiction. But following the fall of the Communist regime, the street came to be named after Ivan Mazepa (1640–1709), the last Cossack ruler of a briefly independent state of Ukraine.[58]

A little alley off the main street has now been named after Bruno Schulz, but as would be appropriate for this shy and withdrawn man, the sign is almost hidden under a large colorful ad for a café-restaurant. From this spot, a little further down across the street, one could still see in June 2004 a handsome, though derelict, building that took up half a block. A photograph

---

[58] Stryjska Street appears in Bruno Schulz's "The Street of Crocodiles." See *The Complete Fiction of Bruno Schulz*, trans. Celina Wieniewska (New York: Walker and Company, 1989), 5.

FIGURE 16. Drohobych city synagogue, now "Spartak" sports club, 2004.

taken in 1909 identifies the building as the City Synagogue of Drohobych, also featuring a few ghostly figures in dark coats and hats leaning on the structure's walls. A much cheerier re-touched photo-postcard dated 1910 also depicts the synagogue, this time looking on at gay horse carriages and elegant gentle-men with walking canes.[59]

The Communists transformed the city synagogue into the sports club "Spartak," which is still there. But while in summer 2004 one could detect the remnants of the Stars of David under

---

[59] The 1909 photo is in Pastukh, *Vulytsiamy,* between pp. 64 and 65. The 1910 postcard is at "The City Synagogue of Drohobycz," http://diaspora.org.il/chamber%20/pics/drohobyz.htm (accessed December 3, 2006) and http://members.tripod.com/~mikerosenzweig/easteursyn.htm (accessed December 3, 2006).

FIGURE 17. The "Choral" Synagogue in Drohobych, 2004.

the peeling plaster, since then the building has been beautifully renovated, in the course of which all indications of its former Jewish identity have been erased.[60] The much larger Great, or Choral, Synagogue, situated on what is now P. Orlyk Street, looms over the city as a vast, empty shell, threatening to collapse, locked and sealed.[61] A few Hebrew words can still be seen over the main gate and on the interior arcs, and patches of paint still cling to the walls. The synagogue is said to be presently under renovation. As can be glimpsed from pre–World War I

[60] See "Synagogues in Drohobycz (Drogobych, Drohobytsch)," http://polishjews.org/synag/drohobycz2.htm (accessed December 3, 2006).

[61] Pylyp Orlyk (1672–1742) succeeded Ivan Mazepa as Ukraine's exiled hetman after the loss of Ukrainian autonomy.

photographs, restoring the exterior, let alone the opulent interior, of this splendid edifice, will be an extraordinarily difficult task.[62]

The site (along with nearby Boryslav) of a great oil boom in the latter nineteenth century and also known for its rich salt mines, Drohobych proudly displays its beautiful sixteenth-century wooden St. George Church, presents some charming old villas surrounded by lovingly tended gardens, and can generally be described as a tidy and elegant town gradually recovering from years of oblivion under Soviet rule in a semisealed borderland security region.[63] But it has erased almost its entire Jewish past.

[62] The photos are in Pastukh, *Vulytsiamy*, between pp. 64 and 65.

[63] See, e.g., "Drohobycz Administrative District: The Petroleum Industry" http://www.shtetlinks.jewishgen.org/Drohobycz/dz_histoil.htm (accessed December 3, 2006); Frank, *Oil Empire*.

Stryi / Stryj / Stryia / Stray

FIGURE 18. The Great Synagogue, Stryi, 2004.

THE SAME can be said for the town of Stryi, which had a population of approximately 11,000 Jews and about 25,000 Poles and Ukrainians in the early 1930s.[64] Before withdrawing from the

[64] *Pinkas Hakehillot*, 383; "Stryy (Stryj), Ukraine," http://www. shtetlinks. jewishgen.org/stryy/ (accessed December 3, 2006); Kamil Barański, *Przeminęli zagończycy, chliborobi, chasydzi: Rzecz o ziemi stanisławowsko-kołomyjsko-stryjskiej* (London: Panda Press, 1988), 219–75, section translated by Ed Talmus, http://www.shtetlinks.jewishgen.org/stryy/stryj-history.html (accessed December 3, 2006). According to Wikipedia, S.V. "Stryi," http://en.wikipedia. org/wiki/Stryi (accessed December 3, 2006), the city numbered close to 31,000 inhabitants in 1931 and 63,000 in 2001.

city in late June 1941 the Soviets murdered many political prisoners in the local jail, including several former Zionist activists. This did not prevent local Ukrainians and Poles, who blamed the Jews for collaborating with the Communists, from carrying out a major pogrom in which many were murdered. Deportations to Bełżec began in May 1942 and lasted until the final liquidation of the Stryi ghetto, on May 22, 1943. On that day the area was surrounded by German soldiers, gendarmes, and Ukrainian militiamen, who were reinforced by men from nearby Drohobych, located a few miles northwest of Stryi. In the course of the *Aktion*, more than a thousand Jews were crammed into the Great Synagogue and kept locked inside it for several days. Many died there for lack of food and water and from the terrible congestion. The rest were taken out and shot at the Jewish cemetery. The imprisoned Jews scraped the walls of the synagogue with their nails, demanding vengeance for their murder.[65]

The Great Synagogue is now an empty shell near the main marketplace. In the summer it is reminiscent of a scene from Gabriel García Márquez's mythical Macondo in his novel *One Hundred Years of Solitude*. But the metamorphosis of this edifice from a house of God into a well-contained minijungle has unintentionally created a memorial to sixty years of silence.[66]

---

[65] *Pinkas Hakehillot*, 390–92. For a history of Jewish Stryi and accounts from the Holocaust, see A. Bar-Lev et al., *The Book of Stryj* (Tel Aviv: Association of Former Stryj Residents in Israel, 1962, in Hebrew with English summary); Yitzhak Nusenblat, *The Mute Cry: The History of the Jews of Stryj, Eastern Galicia, Poland, during World War II* (Tel Aviv: Bamot le'Sifrut ule'Omanut, 1988, in Hebrew), both are available at http://yizkor.nypl.org/index.php?id=2312 (accessed December 3, 2006). An English translation of selected passages can be found at http://www.jewishgen.org/yizkor/stryj2/stryj2.html (accessed December 3, 2006).

[66] Upon seeing this synagogue one may also be reminded of the Torre Guinigi, "the tower with the trees on top," in the Tuscan town of Lucca. But

The screams of the murdered can no longer be heard, their despair has been blown away by the winds of time, their presence as living human beings with hopes for the future and memories of the past has been erased and forgotten. But the explosion of vegetation from within the bare walls, feeding on a soil that was once the heart of a vibrant community's spiritual existence, transforming the blood of the victims into a thick, impassable growth of bushes and trees gives this desolate spot on the edge of the town's center a magical, if somewhat grotesque, air, to which the local residents seem to have become so accustomed they no longer notice it—if they ever did.

But while Stryi has forgotten this past, erasure has in fact been quite selective. Some elements have been forgotten, others given great prominence. And as a few remainders of an unmentioned past survive just a little while longer, time and neglect are certain to eventually wash them away. The synagogue, for instance, that strange creature blooming out of its own desecration, will not last long and already looks more like some ancient ruin than a remainder of a past some can still recall. Down the road one can also still see the faded Polish store names emerging from under the peeling façades of the houses. Otherwise, however, one would be hard put to find a link between these few scattered reminders of forgotten communities and the prominent injunctions to remembrance erected in Stryi since 1945.

These injunctions are there for all to see. Until recently, the most prominent had been a Soviet monument, one of innumerable similar memorials erected all over Soviet Russia and its postwar East European empire. Featuring a huge Soviet soldier

---

while this tree-adorned tower rises from the center of a romantic site par excellence—Lucca is also the birthplace of that great romantic composer, Giacomo Puccini—Stryi's synagogue is the epitome of Ukraine's sites of forgetting, of muted melancholy and pain.

holding up a baby, and an even bigger stone column with the names of all the important battles of the Great Patriotic War—as World War II was called in the Soviet era and is still often referred to in Russia and Ukraine—the monument dominates the central square in this little town. The population's response to it in this post-Soviet era of Ukrainian independence seems ambivalent. Despite its massive presence, it has not been torn down, and even in summer 2004, well over a decade after independence, the monument was adorned with wreathes of fresh flowers apparently commemorating local residents who fell as Red Army soldiers.

Indeed, Ukrainian historiography still constructs the Great Patriotic War as a fundamental element of national identity, and the vast majority of Ukrainians perceive World War II as their national martyrdom. Moreover, there is, in fact, a link between the Soviet project to create a memory of the war from which the unique fate of the Jews has been entirely excised, and the new Ukrainian nationalist project of erasing the Holocaust from the memory of the past while glorifying the nation's martyrs, who, among many other great accomplishments, also participated in the genocide of the Jews. That the Soviets exploited elements of local nationalist sentiments to advance their Communist ideological project, while currently local nationalists are presenting Bolshevism as the great historical enemy even as they look back to the war as their great moment of national reassertion, exemplifies the complexities and ambiguities of Ukraine's politics of memory. But on one issue there was and remains little ambiguity: the urgent need to create a historical memory cleansed of Jewish life, fate, and genocide.[67]

[67] Not everyone seems to accept the continued presence of Soviet memorials. On the day I visited Stryi, the monument had been the target of what appeared to be anti-Russian or anti-Soviet graffiti. For the struggle over the memory of the past in postcommunist Ukraine and the differences in its

An older structure which, at the same time, contains a more contemporary meaning is the newly painted National Ukrainian Home, which also houses a branch of the Prosvita (Enlightenment) Society, founded in L'viv in 1868 with the goal of furthering popular culture and education among the Ukrainian population.[68] This handsome building, devoted to the creation and consolidation of Ukrainian nationalism, now carries a new plaque, put up only after the collapse of Communism, which celebrates the centenary of its erection and honors the prominent national Ukrainian figures who spoke here. These include the poet Ivan Franko and Metropolitan Andrei Sheptyts'kyi along with men associated more with fighting and bloodshed such as Symon Petliura and Stepan Bandera.[69] The fact that especially the so-called Banderivtsi (Banderowcy) units loyal to OUN-B and the Ukrainian Insurgent Army (UPA) were deeply complicit in the murder of the Jews and Poles of Galicia (and Volhynia) is obviously not mentioned anywhere.[70] Indeed,

---

reconstruction in Eastern Galicia, West Volhynia, and the less nationalistic regions in central, southern, and eastern Ukraine, see Jilge, "Politics." See also Amir Weiner, *Making Sense of War: The Second World War and the Fate of the Bolshevik Revolution* (Princeton: Princeton University Press, 2002), 191–235; Timothy Snyder, *The Reconstruction of Nations: Poland, Ukraine, Lithuania, Belarus, 1569–1999* (New Haven: Yale University Press, 2003), 202–14; Serhy Yekelchyk, *Stalin's Empire of Memory: Russian-Ukrainian Relations in the Soviet Historical Imagination* (Buffalo, N.Y.: University of Toronto Press, 2004), esp. 88–128.

[68] For more, see Magocsi, *History of Ukraine*, 442–43.

[69] For the evolution of Ukrainian nationalism under German rule, see Frank Grelka, *Die ukrainische Nationalbewegung unter deutscher Besatzungsherrschaft 1918 und 1941/42* (Wisebaden: Harrassowitz Verlag, 2005).

[70] The OUN split in spring 1941 into two competing fractions: the OUN-M headed by Andrii Mel'nyk and the more radical OUN-B headed by Stepan Bandera. On June 30, 1941, immediately after Germany's invasion of the Soviet Union, Yaroslav Stets'ko of the OUN-B proclaimed Ukrainian

a sculpture of Bandera, who was born in the nearby village of Uhryniv Staryi, has been placed in front of the Stryi gymnasium in which he studied in the 1920s.[71] But the definitive "answer" to the Soviet memorial and to all other possible memories of victimhood and martyrdom has only very recently been completed. In July 2005 the new "Memorial Complex to the Freedom Fighters of Ukraine" was unveiled in the yard of the former NKVD prison in Stryi.[72] This is a grandiose and deeply religious set of monuments, heavy with meaning and geared exclusively to commemorating the Ukrainian nationalist victims of Soviet Communism, even as it incorporates symbols of martyrdom often associated with the Jewish victims of the Holocaust—and thus also the local Jewish

---

independence in L'viv. The Germans quickly arrested Bandera and Stets'ko and kept them in prisons and concentration camps until September 1944. Hence Bandera had no direct control over events in Ukraine during that time; nevertheless he served as a model for his followers. Stets'ko's thinking on the issue of Jewish extermination has already been cited. Ukrainian anti-Soviet and anti-Nazi guerrilla forces were renamed UPA in March 1942 and the following year both the OUN-M and the OUN-B formed their own UPA units. In November 1943 the UPA forces came under command of the OUN-B. Initially active in Volhynia, in summer 1944 the UPA turned to Galicia and fought both the Germans and the Soviets with a force of some 100,000 men. The UPA also recruited widely among Ukrainian policemen and former SS-men who participated in the genocide of the Jews, and carried out massive ethnic cleansing operations of Poles, killing forty to sixty thousand Polish civilians in Volhynia in 1943, and about 25,000 Poles in Galicia in 1944. Magocsi, *History of Ukraine*, 621, 626, 634–35; Snyder, *Reconstruction of Nations*, 162, 170, 176.

[71] The site "STRYI" http://stryi.com.ua/index.php?set_albumName= posts&id=Pam_Banderi&option (accessed December 3, 2006) has a changing gallery of photographs from Stryi that included a photo of this monument. It has now been removed, either temporarily or permanently.

[72] The comment in the previous note also applies to this memorial.

victims of Ukrainian collaborators and nationalists—into a Christian narrative of national resurrection.[73] Thus, for instance, part of the memorial space is overhung with an iron wreath combining the motifs of barbed wire and Christ's crown of thorns; so as not to miss the point, an oversized statue of Mary holding an emaciated Christ forms the other pole of the complex; and a double cross, one built into the yard's wall and another raised from an elevated stone floor, constitutes the third element of the complex. No wonder that the event was inaugurated by a Greek Catholic priest and other clergy, surrounded by Ukraine's national flags of blue and yellow, and accompanied by women wearing traditional Ukrainian dresses. Thus the city has established its link to a past of martyrdom and heroism, even as it has cleansed itself in a religious rite both of its Communist legacy and of its Jewish inhabitants' mass murder.

This is, of course, not to say that Ukrainians have nothing to mourn but rather to point out that they feel obliged to exclude from that mourning the fate of Jews (and Poles) who were murdered in their midst. To be sure, Ukrainians suffered disproportionately compared to most other nations in World War II and its aftermath. Approximately 4.1 million Ukrainian civilians (of whom 1.9 million were Jews) and 1.4 million soldiers died in the war with Germany; about 3.9 million Ukrainians were evacuated eastward by the Soviet government in 1941–42 as the Germans invaded the USSR, and another 2.2 million were deported by the occupiers to Germany as forced labor. As

---

[73] On the use of the iconic image of the prisoner behind barbed wire in postwar German representations of POWs held captive by the Soviets as a kind of "answer" to the more common association of this image with Jewish and Communist victims of Nazi concentration camps, see Robert G. Moeller, *War Stories: The Search for a Usable Past in the Federal Republic of Germany* (Berkeley: University of California Press, 2001).

a consequence of the civil war between Poles and Ukrainians—in which about 20,000 Ukrainians died in fighting with Poles—and of Soviet "population policies" following the reoccupation of these lands by the Red Army, between 1944 and 1946 close to half a million Ukrainians were "repatriated" from Poland to Soviet Ukraine, and 140,660 were internally deported within Poland in 1947. Finally, and most relevant to the Galician culture of mourning, close to 500,000 Western Ukrainians were deported to Siberia and Central Asia between 1946 and 1949 as UPA family members or supporters, and thousands of UPA fighters were killed, executed, or sent to Gulags, as a brutal response to the nationalist resistance to Soviet rule that continued into the 1950s. This most recent and intimate memory of suffering had to be repressed until after the fall of Communism and is now being given a prominent place in the region's commemorative practice.[74]

The largely forgotten former Jewish inhabitants of Stryi have finally been commemorated. But the modest memorial stone erected in their memory is situated about six miles outside of the city, and was constructed only thanks to the efforts of an outsider. Put up in nearby Holobut (Hołobutów), where many

---

[74] Magocsi, *History of Ukraine*, 638, 651; Snyder, *Reconstruction of Nations*, 194, 204–5; Orest Subtelny, *Ukraine: A History*, 3rd ed. (Toronto: University of Toronto Press, 2000), 483, 489–90. On Ukrainian attempts to build a national history of suffering around the tragedy of the Soviet-directed 1932–33 Ukrainian famine, the Holodomor, and to juxtapose it with the Nazi Holocaust as the symbol of absolute evil, see Johan Dietsch, *Making Sense of Suffering: Holocaust and Holodomor in Ukrainian Historical Culture* (Lund, Sweden: Lund University, 2006). It is also true that each of the narratives by Ukrainians, Poles, and Jews stresses the victimhood of its own nation and often ignores or vilifies the other groups. But it cannot be overemphasized that while Ukrainians and Poles often killed Jews as Jews, such practice was not reciprocated for obvious objective reasons. Hence one cannot speak of equally distorted narratives.

of the Jews of Stryi were murdered, the memorial was installed at the initiative of Professor Adam Zieliński, who was born in Drohobych, was raised in Stryi, and lost his father, the lawyer Dr. Karl Rosenberg, in a mass execution of "intellectuals" in Holobut in 1941 (his mother was also subsequently murdered). Zieliński, who moved to Poland after the war and is now a well-known writer living in Vienna, was assisted by Mark Maldis of Polish Television in finally putting up this memorial stone in June 2001, sixty years after the first massacre.[75] This single indication of the fate of Stryi's Jewish community, located in a distant open field, consigns the memory of Jewish life and death to a site outside the perimeter of modern Stryi; it is explicitly meant not for the current inhabitants, but for the Jewish survivors and for family members of the victims. It is unlikely that most people in town even know of this memorial's existence.

The people of Holobut, however, do know. As Mark Maldis writes in the Polish magazine *Trybuna*, whenever it rains in the region, the earth is washed off the shallow graves, and skulls and bones are revealed. Conversely, the population of Stryi discovered the remains of NKVD victims in the former prison only in the early 1990s. Initially skulls into which nails had been driven were exhibited in order to expose Soviet savagery. It took fifteen years to raise the money for the monument commemorating these victims. Lack of funds also seems to have led to the abandonment of the plan to turn the Great Synagogue of Stryi

---

[75] For more information, photographs, and articles related to Zieliński, the history of Stryi, and the erection of the memorial, see "Stryy (Stryj), ukraine," http://www.shtetlinks.jewishgen.org/stryy/ (accessed December 3, 2006) and "Memorial to the martyrs of Holobotow," http://www.shtetlinks.jewishgen.org/stryy/holobotow/zielinski-intro.html (accessed December 3, 2006). See also Adam Zieliński, *Werkausgabe in zehn Bänden* (Klagenfurt: Wieser, 2004); and his *Hołobutów: Dwa opowiadania—Hołobutów: Zwei Erzählungen* (Cracow: Wydawn. Edukacyjne, 1998).

into a public swimming pool.[76] Thus remnants of the past, whether they have always been in public view or suddenly resurface after decades of oblivion, are given different meaning and put to different uses: some serve to reassert martyrdom and identity; some are hurriedly covered up again; and some await their turn to be transformed into more user-friendly structures or to be finally obliterated by time and erosion.

[76] See "Mark Maldis Reveals Secrets of the Criminal Genocide in Holobut," http://www.shtetlinks.jewishgen.org/stryy/holobotow/Trybuna.html (accessed December 3, 2006), and private communication with Sofia Grachova January 30, 2006.

FIGURE 19. The Great Synagogue in Bolekhiv, 2004, as a former tanners' club.

Bolekhiv / Bolechów / Bolekhov / Bolikhov

JUST A FEW MILES south of Stryi, at the foot of the Carpathian Mountains, lies the town of Bolekhiv. Founded in the early seventeenth century, by 1890 Bolekhiv had a population of 4,237 people, of whom three-quarters were Jews. Like many other towns in the region, Bolekhiv declined in the years leading to World War I and during the interwar period. In 1931 it contained close to 3,000 Jews, though the numbers seem to have gone up following the German attack on Poland in 1939. The Soviet withdrawal from the town in July 1941 was followed by several Ukrainian-led pogroms. The Germans took direct control over Bolekhiv in August and by the fall of 1941 the murder of the Jews was well underway, first by mass shootings in the nearby forest and then, as of August 1942, by means of deportations to the Bełżec extermination camp. Ukrainian militias and conscripted Soviet prisoners of war reportedly took an active part in the killing. Following the liberation in August 1944, the Soviet authorities converted the Great Synagogue into a warehouse and completely neglected the Jewish cemetery, in which a mass grave was located.[77]

---

[77] *Pinkas Hakehillot*, 72–79. One of the town's most illustrious sons was Dov-Ber Bolikhover, who spoke Polish, German, Hungarian, Italian, French, and Latin, and was known both for his great Jewish learning and for his public functions. Dov-Ber served as the official interpreter of the representative of the Jews in the public debate between the Frankists (followers of the Shabbatean Jacob Frank [1726–91] who claimed to be the Jewish messiah)

There is no record of this past anywhere in the present-day town of Bolekhiv, which now numbers over 10,000 inhabitants.[78] In June 2004, when I visited it, the only visible remnant of Jewish civilization in Bolekhiv was the Great Synagogue, whose sorry state indicated that it would not remain there for long.[79] The handsome edifice, which appears to have been constructed in the eighteenth century, now bears the Ukrainian inscription, "The Tanners' Club," a somewhat ironic reference to the prewar predominance of the Jews in that trade. Peeping into this locked building one can still see a few remaining stained-glass windows. The turquoise blue paint of the walls

and the Jews in Lemberg (L'viv) in 1759. He also famously responded to an anti-Jewish manifesto published by a priest in Lublin in 1753. Ibid., 73; Wikipedia, S.V. "Jacob Frank," http://en.wikipedia.org/wiki/Jacob_Frank (accessed December 3, 2006). See also Yonah and Mosheh-Hanina Eshel, eds., *Memorial Book for the Martyrs of Bolikhov* (Haifa: Association of Former Bolikhov Residents in Israel, 1957, in Hebrew and Yiddish), http://yizkor.nypl. org/index.php?id=2312 (accessed December 3, 2006); partial English translation available at http://www.jewishgen.org/yizkor/bolekhov/bolekhov.html (accessed December 3, 2006). For photos of the cemetery in its present condition, see "The Cemetery," http://bolechow.ajmendelsohn.com/html/ cemetery.html (accessed December 3, 2006).

[78] Encyclopedia of Ukraine, S.V. "Bolekhiv," http://www.encyclopediaofukraine. com/pages/B/O/Bolekhiv.htm (accessed December 3, 2006).

[79] Some photos of the synagogue and town can be seen at "Bolechow," http://bolechow.ajmendelsohn.com/html/bolechow.html (accessed December 3, 2006) and "Bolekhov; Ukraine," http://www.shtetlinks.jewishgen.org/ bolekhov/index.htm (accessed December 3, 2006). See also the debate over the article by Daniel Mendelsohn, "What Happened to Uncle Shmiel?" *New York Times Magazine*, July 14, 2002, http://www.nytimes.com/ (accessed December 3, 2006), over his visit to Bolekhiv, and especially expressions of anger and frustration by contemporary Ukrainians, at "Prejudice against Ukrainians in NY Times," http://zustrich.quebec-ukraine.com/news02_shmul.htm (accessed August 17, 2006). See now also Mendelsohn, *The Lost: A Search for Six of Six Million* (New York : HarperCollins, 2006).

and pillars may date to a more recent use of the structure. But it seems that by now even the local tanners have abandoned it. One can only assume that sooner or later the former synagogue will be pulled down or will simply disintegrate. Located a short distance from the freshly painted pink and red municipal building with its elegant clock tower, and the Greek Catholic church with its shimmering silver dome, this old sore and the discomforting memories it may still evoke is clearly destined to vanish.[80]

[80] See also Anatol Regnier, *Damals in Bolechów: Eine jüdische Odyssee* (Munich: Goldmann, 1997).

Ivano-Frankivs'k / Ivano-Frankovsk / Stanyslaviv / Stanisławów / Stanislev / Stanislau

Figure 20. The Great Synagogue in Ivano-Frankivs'k, 2004.

Heading southeast of Bolekhiv we come to Stanyslaviv, in 1962 renamed Ivano-Frankivs'k after the poet Ivan Franko. Now the capital of Ivano-Frankivs'k Oblast', the city boasts a population of over 204,000, making it the third largest city in the region after L'viv and Ternopil'. Founded in the mid-seventeenth century, by the end of the nineteenth century the city had a population of 30,000 people, about half of whom were Jews. This ratio declined in the next few decades, so that by 1931 the Jews comprised just over a third of a total population of 72,000.[81]

The Soviet occupation of the city saw the initial appointment of some local Jewish Communists to key positions in the administration. Once the region was annexed formally to the Soviet Ukrainian Republic, however, most positions were taken up by officials from the interior of the USSR. As happened throughout the areas occupied by the Soviets in 1939, the Jewish community and its institutions were broken up, many political activists and business owners were tried and deported, and most businesses were nationalized. In 1940 numerous Jewish refugees from German-occupied Poland were deported to Siberia, Kazakhstan, and other distant territories in the Soviet Union.

[81] This account is based primarily on *Pinkas Hakehillot*, 359–76, English trans., http://www.jewishgen.org/yizkor/pinkas_poland/pol2_00359.html (accessed December 3, 2006). See also *Wikipedia*, S.V. "Ivano-Frankivsk," http://en.wikipedia.org/wiki/Ivano-Frankivsk (accessed December 3, 2006). This site provides very different figures for the 1931 Polish census: Poles: 120,214 (60.6%); Ukrainians: 49,032 (24.7%); Jews 26,996: (13.6%); Total: 196,242. Since the Polish government wanted to stress the success of its Polonization policies in the region, it is possible that there was a fair amount of gerrymandering in this census by including Polish villages around the city and excluding Ukrainians and Jews. See also the full census record, "1931 Polish Statistics Population by Language," http://www.halgal.com/1931popbylang.html (accessed December 3, 2006), which clearly indicates that the figures for all towns include the surrounding population rather than only the urban population. The Polish administrative district of Stanisławów (excluding the city population) on the eve of World War II comprised 600,000 people, of whom 70 percent were Ukrainians, 20 percent Jews, and the remainder made up of smaller local ethnic groups (Górals, Hutsuls, Lemkos, etc.) speaking dialects related to Polish and Ukrainian. Conversely, the city had only a minority of Ukrainians. See Elisabeth Freundlich, *Die Ermordung einer Stadt namens Stanislau: NS-Vernichtungspolitik in Polen 1939–1945* (Vienna: Österreichischer Bundesverlag, 1986), 21.

The Germans took over the city in late July 1941, following a brief Hungarian occupation. The Jewish population numbered at that point about 40,000 people, including refugees from Poland, the Carpathians, and from nearby villages terrorized by the local Ukrainians. An initial execution of several hundred members of the Jewish "intelligentsia" was followed in October by the mass murder of about 10,000 Jews in a single day on the grounds of the "new cemetery."[82] Mass killing resumed in March 1942 until the city was declared *Judenrein* in late February 1943. The few remaining labor camps existed for several more months. The city was liberated by the Red Army in July 1944, but only about a hundred Jews were still alive; another 1,500 survived mainly in the Soviet Union.

Visitors to Ivano-Frankivs'k will find it hard to believe that it has witnessed such massacres. The town boasts beautifully preserved Armenian, Orthodox, Greek Catholic, and Roman Catholic churches, an elegant statue of the poet Adam Mickiewicz, and a tastefully renovated town center with many handsome Habsburg-era houses (beyond the city center many of the streets are still in poor condition). The only surviving edifice from the once large and prosperous Jewish community is the Great Synagogue, which has lost its four onion-domed steeples but remains an impressive structure. The building was handed back to the city's Jewish community following the fall of Communism in 1991. While membership of the synagogue is said to stand at 300, only a few appear to be actively involved.[83] The

---

[82] Pohl, *Judenverfolgung*, 144–47; Sandkühler, *"Endlösung,"* 150–52; Freundlich, *Stanislau*, 154–64; Avraham Liebesman, *With the Jews of Stanislawow in the Holocaust*, trans. Yosef Cohen (Tel Aviv: Ghetto Fighters' House, 1980, in Hebrew), 22–31.

[83] For photos and information, see "Ivano Frankivsk, Ukraine," http://www.shtetlinks.jewishgen.org/Stanislawow/syn.htm (accessed December 3, 2006).

FIGURE 21. Ivano-Frankivs'k memorial to OUN members executed in November 1943 (photo credit: Sofia Grachova, 2006).

synagogue now shares the premises with a store that carries the incongruous name "Universal," and must therefore be entered only through an unmarked backyard, from which one climbs a dark staircase leading to a side entrance into the still impressive, but almost entirely bare, main space of the synagogue. When I visited the town in March 2003, only four middle-aged and elderly men were conducting a service there, far fewer, that is, than a minyan, the minimum quorum of ten men required by Jewish tradition for communal prayer.

Recently a memorial statue has been installed in front of the synagogue. In June 2004 this quasi-abstract bronze figure of a man whose hands are tied behind his back was adorned with fresh wreaths in the Ukrainian national colors of blue and yellow and the black-and-red colors of the UPA. There was no inscription on the memorial, but it was obviously intended to commemorate Ukrainian nationalist victims and perceived as such by the population and the authorities. Since then the monument has been completed with a cross, a Ukrainian trident, and a text indicating that indeed it was erected to commemorate twenty-seven OUN members executed there by the Germans in November 1943.[84] That the Germans chose to shoot Ukrainian patriots against the wall of the synagogue may indicate their own warped perspective. But those who recently erected this monument seem to have been at best entirely oblivious of the implication of remembering "their own" without any indication at the site of the Great Synagogue—or at any other site in the center of town—of the mass murder of Ivano-Frankivs'k's Jewish population. Indeed, rather than constituting a clumsy attempt to unite both communities' memories of victimhood, the monument in all likelihood must be seen as yet another assertion of the

[84] In the photo of this execution included here the wall of the synagogue is clearly visible in the background. The photo appears also in Subtelny, *Ukraine*, in a section of photos between pages 572 and 73, and in Boshyk, *Ukraine during World War II*, in a section of photos between pages 108 and 109. The tourist site "Discover Ukraine" has the following interesting paragraph on the execution and the killing of other "peaceful citizens" without mentioning their identity: "During World War II the city was occupied by fascist troops for three years (1941–1944). The underground representatives of the Organization of Ukrainian Nationalists, Ukrainian Insurgent Army were in charge of the struggle with occupants. The hearts of people are still aching when they recall the public execution of 27 patriots in the center of the city in November 17, 1943. In Stanyslaviv and its suburbs fascists killed more than 100 thousand peaceful people in total." See "Ivano-Frankvisk (Ivano-Frankivska Obtast)," http://tourism.pcukraine.org/info.php?site=Ivano-Frankivsk&oblast=Ivano-Frankivska&PHPSESSID=838b2e94154ded958a77c2a936586a94 (accessed December 3, 2006).

FIGURE 22. Ivano-Frankivs'k execution of UPA members, November 1943 (from Yury Boshyk, *Ukraine during World War II*).

predominance of Ukrainian memory and a negation of any distinct Jewish victimhood, or in fact a complete denial of the historical reality or significance of such victimhood.[85]

[85] The unpublished diary of Viktor Petrykevych, who lived in Ivano-Frankivs'k and Buchach during the German occupation, includes the following entry: "November 18, 1943: Horrible news has reached us. In Stanyslaviv the German police surrounded the theater, searched [gymnasium] students and citizens who were at the theater, and found revolvers on thirty-eight [illegible] of them. [Without delay, the police] shot them at the theater, in front of their acquaintances and friends. People say that the Poles had planted the weapons there and then informed the Gestapo. Other people say that the students were Banderivtsi." Because the theater is across the street from the synagogue and the dates agree with each other, this must be the same execution, although the number cited in the diary is different and the photo shows several men being shot right next to the external wall of the synagogue. Thanks to Sofia Grachova for updating me on this memorial and supplying photos, as well as finding and translating sections from this extraordinary diary.

The cemetery in which the notorious "bloody Sunday" massacre of October 1941 took place is not easy to find; in the local city map the site is confusingly marked with a cross. No signs anywhere in town lead to it or indicate what took place there. The area is overgrown and neglected; many of the tombstones have been removed. A sign at the entrance written only in Hebrew and English announces that the "cemetery was restored with the help of Mr. Emanuel Schaefer from Israel" in memory of his parents and his three sisters who died in the Holocaust. Only one official memorial stone can be found at the site, clearly dating back to the Soviet era and inscribed only in Ukrainian. The inscription reads: "At this site in 1941–44 the German-fascists executed over 100,000 Soviet citizens and prisoners of other lands." As was commonly the practice in all Communist countries, the Jewish identity of the vast majority of the victims is not mentioned. Apart from several smaller memorials put up by family members of the murdered, as well as tombstones of people who died after the war and wished to be buried next to their loved ones, there is only one central post-Soviet memorial to the Jewish community. This modest pink stone, which does not bear the marks of any official participation and must have been put up by private initiative, carries a Star of David and inscriptions in Hebrew, English, and Ukrainian. But while the Hebrew and English inscriptions read, "In memory of 120,000 Jews, victims of the Holocaust 1941–1944," the Ukrainian text dispenses with any mention of Jews and reads instead: "In memory of 120,000 devoured in the Holocaust, 1941–1944." Nowhere is there a description of what in fact happened at this very site or any further details on the extermination of the city's Jews, let alone information about the participation of local collaborators in the massacre.

Kolomyia / Kołomyja / Kolomey / Kolomea

FIGURE 23. Open market in Kolomyia on the site of the Great Synagogue, 2004.

TRAVELING SOUTHEAST of Ivano-Frankivs'k toward the Prut River and the old border with the neighboring province of Bukovina—once part of Romania but now at the southwestern edge of Ukraine—we come to the town of Kolomyia, nestled at the foot of the Carpathian Range. Now numbering some 62,000 people,[86] the city was established in the late fourteenth century, and by the late nineteenth century had become a

---

[86] See "All-Ukrainian Population Census 2001," http://ukrcensus.gov.ua/eng/results/general/city/ (accessed December 3, 2006).

prosperous provincial capital. Despite severe damage and demographic losses in World War I, by the 1930s the population had increased to over 41,000 inhabitants, including Poles, Ukrainians, Hutsuls, Germans, Armenians, Hungarians, Vlachs, and others.[87] Jews had lived in Kolomyia since the fifteenth century, and numbered about 15,000 people on the eve of World War II.

Kolomyia came under direct German control in August 1941, and mass killings began in the fall. Close to 3,000 Jews were shot in a nearby forest in October, and several hundred more in November. Other mass killings claimed the lives of nearly 2,000 people during the winter. In March 1942 some 18,000 Jews were crammed into a ghetto (this statistic obviously includes Jews from surrounding communities), and starting in April the population was subjected to periodic raids in which thousands were taken to Bełżec and hundreds shot on the streets. In November German and Ukrainian troops broke into the ghetto and killed an estimated 5,000 on the spot, along with 1,000 who were executed in the forest. In December Kolomyia was declared *Judenrein*. A further 1,500 Jews were eventually seized by the Germans and the local population in the city and the forests, and were murdered in February 1943. The city was liberated in March 1944 but recaptured by the Germans, only to be finally taken over by the Red Army in August. Very few of its Jewish inhabitants survived, and even after the Germans had left Jews in the region were being murdered by local Ukrainian nationalist bands.[88]

[87] Wikipedia, S.V. "Kolomea," http://en.wikipedia.org/wiki/Kolomea (accessed December 3, 2006). The following account is based primarily on *Pinkas Hakehillot*, 463–76, esp. 472–76.

[88] See also Dov Noi and Mordekhai (Mark) Schutzman, eds., *Memorial Book to the Kolomyia Community and Its Region* (Tel Aviv: Association of Former Residents of Kolomyia and Its Region in Israel and the Diaspora, 1972, in Hebrew), http://yizkor.nypl.org/index.php?id=2312 (accessed December 3, 2006);

There is no record of any of this in present-day Kolomyia. At the site on which the Great Synagogue (Hoykhe Shul) stood until World War II there is a modern building and an open marketplace. There is no sign anywhere to indicate what became of the town's Jewish community. As in Ivano-Frankivs'k, a non-Jewish memorial has in fact been erected next to where the synagogue had stood. This too is a quasi-realistic statue, made of white stone and depicting two women dressed in traditional Ukrainian garb and holding an infant. No plaque indicates what the statue commemorates, but it doubtlessly represents Ukrainian victimhood and must be seen as such by the local population. Kolomyia does have one "functioning" synagogue, a small building on one of the side streets, but it is difficult to tell to what extent it is actually being used. When I visited the town in June 2004, the doors were locked.

In the fall of 1880 Kaiser Franz Joseph visited Kolomyia (known as Kolomea in German) as part of an extensive tour of Eastern Galicia. He was welcomed by the different ethnic groups that made up the city and its surroundings. The Carpathian Hutsuls paraded in their traditional garb. The Jews, who made up over half the total population of 23,000, came out en masse to greet the Habsburg ruler.[89] At the end of World War II the vast majority of their descendents—those who had not emigrated in the intervening period—were lying in mass

English translation, http://www.jewishgen.org/yizkor/kolomyya1/kolomyya.html (accessed December 3, 2006); and Shlomo Bickel, ed., *Pinkas Kolomey: Geshikhte, Zikhroynes, Geshtalten, Khurben* (New York: Kolomeyer Memorial Book / Aaron Hissler, 1957, in Yiddish), http://yizkor.nypl.org/ index.php?id= 2312 (accessed December 3, 2006). For a memoir see "Additional Readings."

[89] On the Kaiser's visit to Kolomyia, see Patrice M. Dabrowski, " 'Discovering' the Galician Borderlands: The Case of the Eastern Carpathians," *Slavic Review* 64, no. 2 (Summer 2005): 380–402. See also Frank, *Oil Empire*, 24–25.

FIGURE 24. Statue at the site of the Great Synagogue, Kolomyia, 2004.

graves in the forests around their town or had been transformed into ashes in the extermination camps. The town does not remember them; they have been wiped clean from the local memory and exist only in the recollections of the few survivors and their offspring, for whom Kolomyia is now a foreign country. Instead, as recently reported, Kolomyia is becoming the base of a new ski industry being developed in the Carpathian

Mountains after decades of neglect by the Soviet authorities. As enterprising young Ukrainians are scouring the slopes in hopes for profit, trendy young tourists are descending on this pristine and cheap corner of Europe. Very few will know that they are treading on the graves of thousands. Not even a reporter from the *New York Times* seems to have had any inkling of this past when he filed his story about this new hopeful development in the farthest reaches of Eastern Europe.[90]

There is no simple explanation for such extraordinary historical amnesia. Some of it, as suggested earlier, has to do with the fact that much of the population of towns such as Kolomyia has neither personal memories nor memories transmitted through families of the mass killing in their town and of its former identity as a Jewish shtetl.[91] Many of the people who inhabit these towns or their ancestors came from elsewhere: they moved into the center of town (and into abandoned Jewish homes) from the surrounding countryside, they were deported into the region from far-off places, or, finally, they came from the interior of the Soviet Union. This also made the process of intentional erasure easier: history textbooks, tourist guides, and journalistic accounts of these regions could tell a distorted history with little fear of being contradicted. The people whose history was being erased were no longer there to protest its

[90] Otto Pohl, "Ukraine Sees Bright Future on Ski Slope," *New York Times*, March 6, 2006.

[91] Yehuda Bauer, "Buczacz and Krzemieniec: The Story of Two Towns during the Holocaust," *Yad Vashem Studies* 33, (2005): 245, defines such a shtetl or "Jewish township" in the former Polish borderlands, or *kresy*, as "an urban settlement that had a population of 1,000 to 15,000 Jews, who constituted at least 35 percent of the total population," as well as having an "organized community life as determined by the Jewish calendar and by the continuity of Jewish tradition within the communal organization of the community," including "a wide variety of welfare, health, educational, religious, and mutual-aid frameworks."

87

erasure; the people who had taken their place had no knowledge of that past and no great desire to find out whose houses they had taken over.

There were, of course, those who had taken part in the extermination of the Jewish communities or had witnessed it. During the years of Soviet rule such people were unlikely to talk much about their collaboration with the Nazis, or their passive complicity. The few who had actually sheltered Jews were just as unlikely to speak about their actions. Former perpetrators could expect punitive action by the authorities, not so much for killing Jews as for collaborating with the "fascists" and for disloyalty to "Soviet power." Former rescuers could expect hostility from the majority of the population, which by and large supported the "removal" of the Jews from its midst and subsequently felt that the fact that there were those who had tried to save the victims reflected badly on themselves. This predilection for ostracizing "good-doers" precisely because their actions serve as an implicit condemnation of those who did not do good, were complicit in evil, or profited from the crime is quite common.[92] Thus for several decades there was little opportunity to speak about the Jewish past of such towns or the manner in which the Jews were murdered.

Since the fall of Communism and Ukrainian independence, it has finally become possible to speak about those who were previously seen by the Soviets as collaborators with the "fascists" and betrayers of the "Soviet nation" as national heroes and the crucial link in the chain of Ukrainian struggle for national liberation. Associating such people with genocide was hardly appropriate. Moreover, the very concept of a newly

---

[92] For an example from Buchach, see Bartov, "Les relations interethniques à Buczacz," 47–67, esp. 59–60; for an example from Jedwabne, see Gross, *Neighbors*, 129–30.

independent Ukraine does not have much room for a memory of regions in which the predominant urban population and much of the cultural and economic influence was wielded by Poles and Jews. Hence, whereas one aspect of the past has emerged from Soviet repression, another has remained in obscurity. Worse still, those who were presented by the Soviets as villains reemerged as heroes and martyrs, while those who were subsumed by the Soviets as "innocent Soviet citizens" have to be concealed even more strenuously by the new nationalist discourse precisely because the villains-turned-martyrs were so often their executioners. And, finally, with the fall of Communism, old popular and traditional anti-Semitism could also reemerge, combining Soviet anti-Jewish imagery with local and religious prejudices that defined the former Jewish populations of these towns as never truly belonging to them—an alien, unpleasant, exploitative, disloyal, strange, and threatening element, even if at times exotic and vaguely fascinating. In other words, the Jews have come to be seen not as a permanent aspect of Galician life, as old and as inherent to what Galicia was as any other population, but as a transitory entity that came and went but had little to do with the "essence" of the existence of Ruthenians/Ukrainians in their ancestral lands.

That many local residents are not able to articulate their views of Jews or more specifically of the Jewish communities that once lived in their towns in this manner is obvious; but I would suggest that any conversation, casual or more in depth, with laypersons or with more educated individuals, will more often than not include at least some of the elements I mentioned.[93]

[93] The Ukrainian historian Yaroslav Hrytsak recently described how his teenaged father was complicit in the murder of a Jew near Stryi in 1942 or 1943. The father recounted this story only in the mid-1990s. For Hrytsak, this "expresses a common pattern of historical memory of Ukrainians in Galicia,

where the Holocaust is underrepresented or even totally absent." Hrytsak's family also did not speak about relatives who were involved with local Ukrainian nationalists. "There were whole layers of memory that was silenced for reasons of my security . . . [and] career. . . . Still," he emphasizes, "the Holocaust was and to a large extent remains one of the most silenced subjects in historical memories of Ukrainians." He explains this as a result of "an overshadowing of the Holocaust by the memories of Soviet persecution and hardships of . . . survival under the Nazi regime," by "a persistence of the theory that Jews were at least partially responsible for their suffering," and by "a widespread belief that Jews exaggerated Ukrainian responsibility for the Jewish extermination." Such views, Hrytsak argues, characterize Ukrainian immigrants in North America, the older generations in Western Ukraine, and a "significant part of the Ukrainian-speaking intellectuals," in other words, "national conscious Ukrainians." Moreover, partly because the Soviet regime silenced the specificity of the Jewish Holocaust, Hrytsak found in interviews with local Western Ukrainians that "even in family stories reminiscences about the Holocaust occupied a marginal role." This was also due to the fact that "when people . . . remembered . . . details of the mass murders . . . places of executions, those who participated in the Jewish extermination, or . . . those who rescued Jews . . . there were no survivors to be seen." These events were even more abstract for the younger generations because "they rarely had a chance to meet any Jewish survivors." Hence, "both the official ideological clichés and family memories excluded any active identification . . . with the issue of the Holocaust." In post-Soviet Ukraine, according to Hrytsak, Ukrainian "national identity is very vulnerable," and therefore "every attempt of a critical reassessment of [Ukraine's] historical past is considered as an attack on their identity. The history of the Holocaust provokes such a situation. Therefore Ukrainians tend either to silence those stories, or to repudiate them." Hrytsak rightly insists that remembering the Holocaust rather than suppressing its memory "could help [Ukrainians] to elaborate a critical perspective of their own history." Yaroslav Hrytsak, "The Holocaust in Historical Memory of Ukrainians," (paper presented at "The War and the Holocaust in the Collective Memory of Jews, Germans, Poles, Ukrainians, and Lithuanians" conference, Ben-Gurion University, May 17–25, 1998).

Kosiv / Kosów / Kosov / Kosow

FIGURE 25. The "L'vy" (Lions) Company ready for action in 1944 (photo of photo in Kosiv museum, 2004).

As WE DRIVE south of Kolomyia, almost all the way to the border of Bukovina, we reach the town of Kosiv. Surrounded by hills, this pretty one-street town benefits from the mountain air of the Carpathians, and a cool breeze occasionally blows through the lush vegetation even on this warm June day in 2004. Walking down the main street, we soon come upon an elegant two-story nineteenth-century house facing the main town square. The plaques on either sides of the main door describe it as the National Art Museum, dedicated both to "Hutsul Customs" and to "the Struggle for Liberation in Hutsul Lands." It is the latter part of the museum that draws our attention, as well as that of a small group of local tourists.

This exhibit has little to do with the Hutsul ethnic group that inhabits this part of the Carpathians. Rather, what attracts the teenagers and young couples, some with children and babies, to this cramped space, is not an ethnographic but a nationalist exhibit. The guide—an elderly, wiry, tough-looking man—is holding forth. The room is dedicated to the freedom fighters of the region, the troops of UPA. The walls are covered with the photographs of these young, handsome fighters, filled with determination to keep up the hopeless struggle against the Soviet reoccupation of their lands in 1944, in which so many of them died. One cannot help but admire the heroism of these men and lament the tragedy of their fate, even as one wonders about the folly of trying to scare away the army that had just defeated the German Wehrmacht. The youthful visitors seem inspired, and the old man, evidently a veteran UPA fighter, lectures them about the sacrifice of these martyrs.

The men in the photos, however, are mostly dressed in German army uniforms, armed with German weapons, and holding the leashes of fierce German dogs. They may be aware of the impending tragedy, but for now they seem quite happy in fulfilling their tasks, which, as we know, included going out on "Jew hunts" and assisting the Germans in the mass murder of the local Jewish population. One of the photos hits home: in it the "L'vy" (Lions) Company is posing by the banks of the Strypa, a river that loops around the town of Buchach. The date is July 1944, and the men with their German shepherd, field caps, stick grenades, and MG machine guns, look eager for action. It is just sixty years prior to my visit.

Being Jewish—my mother's family left Buchach in 1935—I would not have fared well at the hands of the "L'vy" Company, or for that matter at those of the "Burlaky" Company (photographed in spring 1946 and already equipped with a mix of Soviet and German uniforms and weapons), or of any other unit of UPA freedom fighters. The little Kosiv exhibit does not divulge any of the murkier aspects of the UPA's struggle for independence—liberation from the yoke of Polish rule, German occupation, Soviet oppression, and, as they saw it, Jewish exploitation and collaboration with Ukraine's enemies and oppressors. Nor is it likely that the young visitors who crowded the room had any inkling of the crimes committed by this organization or of the predominant prewar presence of Jews in this very town, where the Jewish population of 2,400 people recorded in 1931 comprised half of the total inhabitants. Indeed, while the exhibit celebrates Ukrainian nationalism and independence, not a single marker in town reminds the present inhabitants of its past. The museum guide surely knew what he and his presumed comrades had been up to during the war. So did the elderly woman at the museum ticket booth. As we were leaving, she must have realized that one of us was a foreigner. Did we know to whom this house had once belonged? No, we answered, somewhat puzzled. This was the rabbi's house, the woman stated, sounding almost relieved to be able finally to disclose this information. She looked as if she could have been a girl during the war.

I did not quite believe her. It seemed all too cynical to house an exhibition for the killers of the Jews in the house of the victims' spiritual leader. Then I looked up Kosiv's memorial book and found there a hand-drawn map, indicating the exact location of the rabbi's house—precisely where the museum is now situated.[94] Facing the rabbi's house in the main town square stands a new three-story city hall, whose bright red roof tiles and pink façade violently clash with the deep green of the steep forested hill in the background. In front of the building is a white sculpture depicting Mother Mary holding baby Jesus.

[94] G. Kresel and L. Olitski, eds., *Yizkor Book of Kehilat Kosow (Kosow Huculski)* (Tel Aviv: Hamenora, 1964, in Hebrew and Yiddish), folded map after title page, http://yizkor.nypl.org/index.php?id=2312 (accessed December 3, 2006).

FIGURE 26. The rabbi's house and museum in Kosiv, 2004.

The Great Synagogue, once famous for its splendor, stood on the left side of city hall, but there is no trace of it. On the right side is another steep, overgrown hill. A closer look reveals that it is dotted with hundreds of tombstones, most half covered with brush or sunken into the rich soil. This is the only surviving evidence of the city's Jewish past, gradually being swallowed into the earth and meanwhile a fertile grazing ground for local goats.

Goats were a main source of trade in nineteenth-century Kosiv, where a successful tanning industry developed alongside the production of salt from fountains in the area. Jews are known to have lived there as of the early seventeenth

FIGURE 27. The Jewish cemetery in Kosiv, 2004.

century.[95] The town underwent some industrialization in the late nineteenth century with the opening of a factory for rugs and blankets. The Jewish community was under religious rule until the late 1930s. But in the first municipal elections of 1928, the three main ethnic groups agreed that Jews would comprise half of the city council. Toward the end of the interwar period the Zionists became the strongest political faction in the town. Secular education, especially for girls, was on the rise, and cultural activities, sports associations, youth groups, and political

[95] The following is based on *Pinkas Hakehillot*, 481–86. See also Yehoshua Gertner and Danek Gertner, *The House is No Longer There: The Destruction of the Jews of Kosów and Żabie*, trans. Rinat Kahanov (Jerusalem: Yad Vashem, 2000, in Hebrew).

95

organizations indicated the rapid transformation of what had been a strict religious community that had produced several important Hassidic figures.

Kosiv was flooded with Jewish refugees fleeing German-occupied Poland in the fall of 1939. When the Soviets retreated in 1941, only a few young Jews managed to escape from Kosiv. The town came under Hungarian occupation and a series of anti-Jewish measures were enacted by the new authorities. In September Kosiv passed over to German control and acts of violence by the occupiers as well as the local Ukrainian population greatly increased. In mid-October 1941 about 2,200 Jews—more than half the community—were murdered, with active participation of the Ukrainian militia and local Ukrainians. The Jews were shot on a hill across the river, their bodies falling into two vast predug pits. The synagogue was set on fire. In spring 1942 some 700 Jews were transferred to the ghetto in Kolomyia, and the Jews who remained in Kosiv were also enclosed in a ghetto. In September some 150 Jews were shot in town and another 600 transported to Bełżec. The last survivors were sent to Kolomyia in November 1942 and Kosiv was declared *Judenrein*. While some Jews were sheltered by gentile neighbors, many others were hunted down by the local population in the forests and murdered. No record of these events is to be found in contemporary Kosiv, and the municipal authorities provide no information.

Kuty / Kitov / Kitev / Kittiv

FIGURE 28. The Jewish cemetery in Kuty, 2004.

GOATS ARE also a common feature in the overgrown Jewish cemetery in Kuty, resting in the afternoon sun amongst the intricately carved tombstones.[96] Some 30 miles south of Kolomyia,

[96] This account is based mainly on *Pinkas Hakehillot*, 460–63, English translation, http://www.jewishgen.org/yizkor/pinkas_poland/pol2_00460.html (accessed December 3, 2006). See also Chaim Zins, ed., *Kitov, My Hometown: Survivors of Kuty Tell the Story of Their Town* (Tel Aviv: Ya'ir, 1993), http://yizkor.nypl.org/index.php?id=2312 (accessed December 3, 2006); English translation of extracts, http://www.spectelresearch.com/PSchattner/Kuty.html (accessed December 3, 2006); Eisig Husen, ed., *Kittever Yiskor Book: A Memorial* (New York: Kittever Sick and Benevolent Society, 1958, in Yiddish),

and only a short drive from Kosiv, this charming little town lies along the banks of the Cheremosh (Czeremosz) River, which separates Galicia and Bukovina and served as the border between Poland and Romania during the interwar period. On the other side of the river, connected by a bridge to Kuty, is the town of Vyzhnytsia (Wiznitz, Vizhnitsa, Vijniţa), once a major Hassidic center whose impressive synagogue has been turned into a cultural center and a theater without a single indication of its previous identity.

Kuty numbered 2,900 Jews in 1931, well over half the population of the town. Following the German attack on the Soviet Union, Kuty was first taken over by Hungarian and Romanian troops, and then passed over to the Germans in September 1941. During the winter of 1941–42 many of its Jews died of epidemics due to lack of food. Those who tried to escape to Romania or forage for food in the forests were murdered by the local population. In April 1942 German SS and Gestapo units accompanied by Ukrainian militia raided the town and murdered close to 1,000 people. Another 500 were deported to Kolomyia, but many were murdered on the way there. In September 1942 another 800 were taken to Kolomyia, from which most were transported to Bełżec and a group of young

---

http://yizkor.nypl.org/index.php?id=2312 (accessed December 3, 2006); Martin Rudner ed., *Kuty: Echoes of a Vanished Heritage*, 1993, http://www. ibiblio.org/yiddish/Places/Kuty/ (accessed December 3, 2006). For a Polish view, see "Stanisłowskie II Rzeczpospolita Pokuele: Kuty," http://rzecz-pospolita. com/kuty0.php3 (accessed December 3, 2006). On the perpetrators in this region, in addition to Pohl, *Judenverfolgung*, and Sandkühler, *"Endlösung,"* see also Christopher R. Browning, *Ordinary Men: Reserve Police Battalion and the Final Solution in Poland* (New York: HarperCollins, 1993), 30–37. On tombstones, see Michael Nosonovsky, *Hebrew Epitaphs and Inscriptions from Ukraine and Former Soviet Union* (Washington, D.C.: Michael Nosonovsky, 2006).

men were sent to the Yaniv (Janowska) concentration camp. The last 18 craftsmen left in Kuty were shot two months later and the town was declared *Judenrein*. The Soviets reoccupied Kuty in April 1944, but very few of its Jewish inhabitants were found alive.

Horodenka / Gorodenka

FIGURE 29. Plaque attached to the Great Synagogue of Horodenka, 2005 (photo credit: Artem Svyrydov).

As WE drive along the former border with Bukovina heading northeast, we arrive at Horodenka, situated some 30 miles northwest of Chernivtsi (Czernowitz).[97] Established as a city in

[97] For the following, see *Pinkas Hakehillot*, 175–81; Shimon Meltzer, ed., *The Book of Horodenka* (Tel Aviv: Association of Former Residents of Horodenka and Its Region, 1963, in Hebrew and Yiddish), available http://yizkor. nypl.org/index.php?id=2312 (accessed December 3, 2006); English translation, http://www.jewishgen.org/yizkor/gorodenka/gorodenka.html (accessed

the seventeenth century, Horodenka had the typical regional mix of Ukrainian, Polish, and Jewish populations. On the eve of World War I the Jews constituted more than a third of the total population of over 11,000 inhabitants.[98] The war caused great damage to the town, and many of its inhabitants fled. But it is estimated that in 1939 there were some 4,000 Jews in Horodenka, soon joined by many refugees fleeing from German-occupied Poland. In July 1941 the town was taken over by Hungarian troops, and the local Ukrainian municipality and militia forced the Jews to wear distinctive markings and abused the population.

In September 1941 the Germans took over, establishing a ghetto in November. The following month some 2,500 Jews were concentrated in the Great Synagogue, from which they were transported about ten miles to the forest between the villages of

---

December 3, 2006). See also Tosia Schneider, "Visiting Horodenka, Fifty-three Years Later," http://www.geocities.com/mrheckman/gorodenka/tschneider.html (accessed December 3, 2006); Tosia Szechter Schneider, "A Horodenka Holocaust Memoir," http://www.geocities.com/mrheckman/gorodenka/bio1a.htm (accessed December 3, 2006). For photos of the former synagogue, see also "Photos from Horodenka, 1992," http://www.geocities.com/mrheckman/gorodenka/pic-solomowitz.html (accessed December 3, 2006); Hebrew-language account by Yad Vashem, http://www1.yadvashem.org/ odot_pdf/ Microsoft%20Word%20-%201145.pdf (accessed December 3, 2006). See also the remarkable account by Tomasz Miedzinski, interviewed by Anka Grupinska in December 2003 and January–February 2004, http://www.centropa.org/ archive.asp?mode=bio&DB=HIST&fn=Tomasz&ln=Miedzinski&country= Poland (accessed December 3, 2006).

[98] Horodenka's population in 2001 was 9,794 people. See *Encyclopedia of Ukraine*, S.V. "Horodenka," http://encyclopediaofukraine.com/display.asp? linkPath=pages\H\O\Horodenka.htm (accessed December 3, 2006), also providing some photos, but not a single word about the city's former Jewish population.

Semakivtsi (Siemakowce) and Mykhal'che (Michałcze) and executed. Following this massacre Jews from the surrounding villages were concentrated in Horodenka. As of April 1942 the remaining Jewish population was either shot at the Jewish cemetery or transported to the Bełżec extermination camp. The ghetto in Horodenka was liquidated in July 1942; those still capable of work were sent to the Yaniv (Janowska) concentration camp and the rest to Bełżec. Young Jews who escaped to the forests found themselves targets of Ukrainian Banderivtsi (Banderowcy) units but are said to have cooperated with Polish self-defense groups, themselves under attacks from the Ukrainian nationalists. A few Jews survived in labor camps and were liberated by the Red Army in March 1944, but even then some of them were killed in a German air raid.

The most distinctive feature reminding us of Horodenka's past is the impressive Roman Catholic Dormition Church (1763) built by the L'viv architect Bernard Meretyn and decorated by the Austrian-L'viv artist Jan Jerzy (Johann Georg) Pinzel, both of whom also built and decorated the famous city hall of Buchach (see more later). The church was badly damaged in World War II, and much of its interior was destroyed. But it is still a magnificent edifice at the center of the town. Conversely, the town contains very few signs of its former Jewish population. The Great Synagogue has been transformed into a school. A plaque attached to it carries the following text in Hebrew, Ukrainian, English, and Yiddish: "This is the site of the Great Synagogue of the Jewish Community that existed from 1742 till 1941. Half of this community of Horodenka and its vicinity were taken from here by the Nazis and murdered on Dec. 4, 1941. May the memory of the Holocaust Martyrs be blessed forever." Interestingly, only the Hebrew and Yiddish texts indicate that the mass killing took place at the village of Semakivtsi.

FIGURE 30. The Great Synagogue of Horodenka, 2005 (photo credit: Artem Svyrydov).

At the Jewish cemetery a memorial was installed some years ago by a local Jewish inhabitant with help from survivors in Israel, without any assistance from the town. Still, its Hebrew and Ukrainian inscriptions differ substantially. The Hebrew text reads: "In remembrance of all the martyrs of Horodenka and the surroundings—victims of the Shoah, who were murdered by the Nazis and their collaborators in roundups [*aktsyot*], labor camps, extermination camps, and in all other ways during World War II, 1941–1945." The Ukrainian text, for its part, refers only to a specific event that took place at the cemetery and makes no mention of collaborators. It reads: "In remembrance of the Jews of Horodenka, who perished in the second roundup, April 12, 1942. Eternal memory to the innocent martyrs, victims of Nazism."[99]

Another memorial stone was put up during the Soviet period at the site of the mass murder in Semakovtsy, hardly an easy spot to find. The memorial carries the simple formula, dedicated, as was common under Communism, "to the victims of fascism." A plaque was added to it after the fall of the Communist regime, inscribed in Hebrew, Ukrainian, English, and Yiddish: "Mass grave of 2,500 Jews—adults and children—from Horodenka and the vicinity who were murdered here by the Nazis on December 4, 1941. May the memory of the Holocaust victims be blessed forever." One doubts, however, that the present inhabitants of Horodenka ever come to this memorial, or that they associate the victims mentioned there with the Jews who had once lived in their town, let alone recall that the killing was accomplished with ample help from the local population.[100]

[99] The memorial uses the term *yevreï*, rather than *zhydy*, suggesting that Jewish survivors prefer this term despite local claims that *zhydy* is a neutral designation for Jews; but this may also be related to Soviet influence. See also n. 46 in this section.

[100] For a German document dated September 14, 1942, that describes the "resettlement" of the Jews of this region, see " 'Judenumsiedlung' in ostgalizien," http://www.ns-archiv.de/verfolgung/polen/ostgalizien/umsiedlung.php (accessed December 3, 2006), including, e.g., the following: "On September 8 and 9, 1942, roundups [*Aktionen*] were carried out in Kuty, Kosow, Horodenka, Zaplatow and Sniatyn. Some 1,500 Jews had to be driven on foot 31 miles from Kuty or 21 miles from Kosow to Kolomea, where they spent the night in the courtyard of the Sipo (Security Police) prison with other Jews brought there from the area. Apart from the Jews seized in Horodenka and Sniatyn, who were already loaded in these sites into 10 railroad cars by the Sipo, another 30 railroad cars were loaded in Kolomea. The total number of the Jews sent with the resettlement train to Belzec on September 10, 1942, reached 8,205" (my translation).

Husiatyn / Gusyatin / Hussiatin / Husiyatan

Figure 31. The Fortress Synagogue of Husiatyn, 2004.

WE CONTINUE from Horodenka due northeast to Husiatyn, on the banks of the Zbruch River, which served as the interwar border between Poland and the Soviet Union. Husiatyn boasts several architectural monuments, including a sixteenth-century church, a fine but derelict early seventeenth-century Bernardine monastery and church, the ruins of a seventeenth-century castle, and a seventeenth-century town hall. The town also has an exquisite late seventeenth-century synagogue built in the Renaissance style, a symbol of the Jewish community's golden age.[101]

[101] The following is based mainly on *Pinkas Hakehillot*, 181–85. See also Abraham Backer, *Two Communities (Husiatyn and Kopyczynce)* (Tel Aviv: Association

Husiatyn was given the status of city in 1559, but in the subsequent decades it came under attacks by the Cossacks and the
Turks. The town began to develop rapidly in the eighteenth century. Following the partition of Poland in 1772, Husiatyn was
divided into two parts as the Zbruch River became the border
between Russian Podolia and Austrian Galicia. The town had a
Jewish population from the very beginning of its existence, and
on the eve of World War I the 3,288 Jewish inhabitants constituted well over half the total population, the remaining inhabitants more or less equally divided between Poles and Ukrainians.
But with the conquest of Husiatyn by the Russian army in 1914
much of the town was destroyed, and most of its inhabitants
fled or were deported. Husiatyn never recovered from the war;
its Jewish population was hit especially hard. In the early 1930s
there were under 400 Jews among approximately 2,000 inhabitants. The town was occupied by the Germans in early July 1941,
and in that first month about 200 Jews were murdered by the
occupiers and their Ukrainian collaborators. In March 1942 the
remnants of the community were deported to other towns in
the region and subsequently perished.

The elegant old Festungs-Schul (Fortress Synagogue) is still
standing on the outskirts of Husiatyn. Under Soviet postwar
rule the synagogue was rather shabbily reconstructed and converted into a museum; it still carries a prominent sign identifying it as such. But while no indication of its previous identity is

---

of Former Residents of Galician Husiatyn in Israel, 1977, in Hebrew and Yid-
dish); Benjamin Diamond, ed., *Husiatin: Podolia (Ukraine): Jewish Settlement
Founded in 16th Century, Annihilated in 1942* (New York: Group of Husiatin
Landsleit in America, 1968, in Yiddish and English). For a memoir see "Addi-
tional Readings." See also "Husiatyn," http://www.shtetlinks.jewishgen.org/
Suchostaw/sl_husiatyn.htm (accessed December 3, 2006); *wikipedia*, S.V.
"Husiatyn," http://en.wikipedia.org/wiki/Husiatyn (accessed December 3,
2006).

provided, and the prominent Star of David that can be seen from old photographs above its main gate has been erased, the structure still looks unmistakably like a Galician synagogue.[102] A survey by the United States Commission for the Preservation of America's Heritage Abroad in the 1990s determined that the building was in relatively good condition.[103] But by the time I visited the synagogue in June 2004 it was in a sorry state. The museum had been closed, and the exhibit, which could only be glimpsed through the broken windows, seemed quite dilapidated, even though it had apparently been redesigned to suit independent Ukraine's newly shaped historical narrative. I could see no indications that the exhibit referred in any way to the original purpose of the building that housed it.

On the hill overlooking the synagogue stands a particularly tasteless Soviet monument commemorating the sixtieth anniversary of the 1917 revolution. Painted with garish colors over a rough cement surface, the monument depicts oversized primitive figures in heroic poses, offering a strange but not untypical mix of Communism and Ukrainian nationalism (the

---

[102] Backer, *Two Communities*, 16, contains a photograph of the Alte Shul taken by the Yiddish poet, dramatist, journalist, editor, and photographer Alter Kacyzne (1885–1941), who was beaten to death by a Ukrainian on July 7, 1941, at the Jewish cemetery in Ternopil'. His death was witnessed by the Yiddish poet Nakhman Blitz, who survived the pogrom. Blitz published an account of his death as "Der Kreyts-veg fun Alter Kacyzne" [The Martyrdom of Alter Kacyzne] in the Yiddish daily *Dos naye lebn* [The New Life] (Łódź), no. 10, (1945). See Alter Kacyzne, *Poyln: Jewish Life in the Old Country*, ed. Marek Web (New York: Metropolitan Books, 1999), xxi–xxii.

[103] See "United States Commission for the Preservation of America's Heritage Abroad: Jewish Cemeteries, Synagogues, and Mass Grave Sites in Ukraine (2005)," 41, http://www.heritageabroad.gov/reports/doc/survey_ukraine_2005.pdf (accessed December 3, 2006). See also "Zamky ta Khramy Ukrainy" [Ukrainian Castles and Church] http://www.mycastles.com.ua/index.php?id=gus (accessed December 3, 2006).

FIGURE 32. Soviet monument to the Revolution, Husiatyn, 2004.

figures wearing a rough approximation of Ukrainian national dress). Here too, no mention whatsoever is made of fate of Husiatyn's prewar Jewish inhabitants. Comparing the elegant edifice of the synagogue with its deteriorating propagandistic content, let alone with the gaudy revolutionary monument looking down on it from the forested hill, one may conclude that despite all pronouncements to the contrary, civilization seems to have made little progress in the three centuries since the synagogue was built.

Chortkiv / Czortków / Chortkov / Tshortkev

FIGURE 33. Gate to demolished Jewish World War I cemetery in Chortkiv, 2004.

FROM HUSIATYN we continue to the city of Chortkiv, which lies slightly to the southwest. Founded as a private city in the mid-sixteenth century, the town suffered a great deal, like many of its neighbors, from wars and foreign occupations during the following century. Ruled after 1772 by the Habsburg Empire (but coming under Russian rule in 1809–15), Chortkiv was occupied by the Russian army for much of World War I and, following a brief period of Ukrainian rule, became part of interwar Poland. It is known to have had a Jewish population since the seventeenth century. By the beginning of the twentieth century its 3,000 Jewish inhabitants constituted more than 60 percent of the population. This ratio steadily declined in the next decades thanks to emigration triggered by economic hardship and war. In 1935 there were close to 6,000 Jews in Chortkiv, but they constituted only 30 percent of the population, in which Poles vastly outnumbered Ukrainians.[104]

Soviet rule in 1939–41 brought with it a great deal of oppression and violence. The usual expropriations of property, changes in the school curriculum, suppression of religion, arrests, and deportations were also accompanied in Chortkiv in January 1940, by an uprising of Polish students which was brutally put down by the Soviets. Up to 600 rebels were rounded up, some were summarily shot, and others were first tried and then executed or imprisoned.[105] The city was occupied by the Germans

[104] This account is based on *Pinkas Hakehillot*, 443–50. See also Yeshayahu Austri-Dunn, ed., *Memorial Book of Czortkow* (Haifa: Association of Former Residents of Czortkow in Israel, 1967, in Hebrew and Yiddish with English summary), English translation, http://www.jewishgen.org/Yizkor/chortkov/Chortkov.html (accessed December 3, 2006); Sidney C. Gelb, *Chortkov Remembered: The Annihilation of a Jewish Community (Ukraine)* (Dumont, N.J.: Self-published, 1990), http://www.jewishgen.org/yizkor/Chortkova/Chortkov.html (accessed December 3, 2006); Florence Mayer Lieblich, *Someone Is Watching Over Me: A Memoir*, http://www.remember.org/florence/print.html (accessed December 3, 2006). See also "Czortkow," http://www.kresy.co.uk/czortkow.html (accessed December 3, 2006), which gives the following population figures based on the census of January 1, 1939: Poles, 10,504; Jews, 4,860; Rusins (Ruthenians), Ukrainians, 3,631; Germans, Russians, Armenians, and others: 220; total: 19,215.

[105] Gross, *Revolution from Abroad*, 139–40, 172. On the discovery of murdered political prisoners with the withdrawal of the Soviets, see 179, 181. See also Jędrzej Tucholski, "Powstanie w Czortkowie—wersja NKWD," *KARTA* 31 (2000): 92–110. On the Soviet massacre of prisoners and the German-led pogrom that followed, see also the account by a Ukrainian who may have witnessed or taken part in these events: Andrii Bazalins'kyi, "Za muramy chortkivs'koï tiurmy" [Behind the walls of the Chortkiv prison], *Vil'ne*

in early July 1941. The discovery of political prisoners who had been murdered by the NKVD in the city jail before the Soviets' retreat unleashed a massive pogrom and the killing of hundreds of Jews. This was followed by organized executions of Jews by the Germans in the nearby Chornyi Lis (in Polish Czarny Las, or Black Forest) in the summer and fall and the recruitment of forced labor to murderous camps in the region. In April 1942 a ghetto was established; the first major *Aktion* took place in August. The entire Jewish population was concentrated in the market square; about 600 people were murdered on the spot while another 2,000 were taken by train to the Bełżec extermination camp. A second *Aktion* in October doomed another 500 people. The ghetto was then reorganized as a labor camp, which in turn was liquidated in June 1943. In September the town was declared *Judenrein.* Only about 100 Jews were still alive in Chortkiv and its surroundings by the time the city was finally liberated by the Red Army in summer 1944.

Chortkiv is located astride the Seret River, which is a tributary of the Dnister. Not far from the town stands the romantic ruin of an early seventeenth-century castle, next to which is a Greek Catholic church. In front of the church a large metal cross adorned with Ukraine's national flag has recently been put up. At the foot of the cross a triumphant plaque praises God's boundless mercy and declares emphatically: "Gone forever are the days of darkness. Long live Ukraine and its free people!" As we head to the center of Chortkiv, we find an eighteenth-century Roman Catholic church towering over the central square. The hallway leading into the church displays framed articles and pamphlets celebrating the beatification by Pope John Paul II of 108 Polish martyrs killed by the Nazis,

---

zhyttia, January 21, 1997, 3–4. Thanks to Marco Carynnyk for drawing my attention to this article.

many of whom were murdered for trying to rescue Jews.[106] This rare commemoration of Polish victimhood on Western Ukrainian soil has no space for the innumerable murdered Jews of Chortkiv. We also learn that under the Communists this impressive edifice was transformed into a storage house. But unlike Jewish sites there and elsewhere, the church has now been renovated and dominates the entire landscape. Indeed, Chortkiv also contains two carefully preserved wooden churches built in the Podolian tradition in the seventeenth and eighteenth centuries.

Why have the religious symbols of two communities whose actual members are almost entirely absent from the region fared so differently? In part, there is little doubt that the local Ukrainian population, whether Greek Catholic or Orthodox (Ukrainian or Russian), maintains a sense of respect for Roman Catholic places of worship, even as it retains a degree of suspicion or hostility toward Jews. Moreover, not only is Poland geographically just across the border, since the fall of Communism it has also experienced a growing interest in the remnants of Polish civilization in what were for many centuries Polish-ruled lands. Hence we find groups of volunteers who come during their vacations to restore churches; it would appear that there is also some financial investment in such undertakings by the Polish Church and the Vatican.

Conversely, as Ukrainians will occasionally say, "the Jews won't pay" for restoring remnants of Jewish civilization in Galicia. Apart from installing some fences around cemeteries or raising "memorial tents" by this or that Hasidic sect for their own rabbi, saving what is left does not seem to be a priority for any Jewish

---

[106] See *Zenit*, June 18, 1999, http://www.zenit.org/english/archive/9906/ ZE990618.html (accessed December 3, 2006); "Beatifications set for Pope's Polish Trip," *Catholic World News*, May 31, 1999, http://www.cwnews.com/ news/viewstory.cfm?recnum=10402 (accessed December 3, 2006).

Figure 34. Chortkiv Roman Catholic church, 2004.

organization. This may reflect the reality that no communities which might benefit from such renovation are left. But it may also indicate a sense among Jews that unlike Catholic churches, synagogues will be seen as an alien feature in what is now a purely Ukrainian landscape, possibly becoming the target of anti-Semitic attacks or at least of anxious conversations about the "return of the Jews." And if Western Ukrainians in particular still harbor anti-Jewish prejudices, many Jews, whether they belong to the dwindling community of survivors or have never been to Ukraine, also tend to associate Ukrainians with pogroms and massacres. They go there, if at all, to see what is left, not to help save it.

Not far from the Catholic church is the city's nineteenth-century market square. When I visited Chortkiv in June 2004

FIGURE 35. Chortkiv marketplace with prewar Jewish store signs, 2004.

the market was under renovation, but the prewar store signs above the shop windows were still visible. It was a matter of sheer luck to have come there that day. The sun was shining, the atmosphere was festive, and the faded Polish and Jewish names painted on the walls could clearly be seen. A few days later and the words would have been neatly painted over and just as quickly forgotten. But on that day, the long dead M. Tauber and Leib Wasserman were still advertising their paint and iron store right next to the "Catholic Butcher."

At the corner of the market a plaque for a nationalist fighter has been placed on the wall. Adorned with fresh flowers, the text reads: "At this site, on February 2, 1945, the organs of the NKVD executed by hanging the UPA hero Il'kiv Hryhoriy

115

'Puhach,' born in Boryshkivtsi, Borshchiv District. Eternal glory to the hero who restored life to free Ukraine." The fierce young face of "Puhach" stares at us from the plaque, sporting a traditional Ukrainian shirt, now finally celebrated for the belated triumph of his cause. Neither "Puhach" nor any of the shoppers crowding the arcade seem to be aware of the fact that at this very spot Chortkiv's Jewish population was concentrated for the first roundups that led to its annihilation by the occupying Germans and their Ukrainian collaborators. Not even the humblest plaque has been put up in the square to commemorate their mass murder, possibly not only because of neglect and lack of interest, but also because remembering the fate of the Jews might cast a shadow over the glory of UPA's heroes, who often participated in the murder of the Jews. It might also serve as an unwelcome reminder that Chortkiv was once known by most of its inhabitants by its Polish or Jewish name, and was a town with a large and thriving Jewish and Polish population living side by side with Ukrainian neighbors.

There are several other new memorials in town, mostly put up after the fall of the Soviet Union. One edifice, made of Ukrainian granite, celebrates the local UPA hero Petro Khamchuk, who was killed in 1948 at the age of twenty-nine. The plaque's golden letters note that "Petro the Nimble" (clearly his underground name) was awarded the Iron Cross, which would seem to indicate that he was also appreciated by the German Wehrmacht during his short military career. Next to the imposing police station building—which during the German occupation served as the headquarters of the Sipo (*Sicherheitspolizei* or Security Police of the SS and SD) outpost that organized the murder of some 60,000 Jews in the Chortkiv region—now stands an anti-Soviet memorial.[107] This somber, cross-shaped

---

[107] Bartov, "Guilt and Accountability in the Postwar Courtroom."

monument, also adorned with fresh flowers, is dedicated to those "Tortured to Death in the Chortkiv Prison in July 1941." Thus it not only mourns and celebrates the Ukrainian nationalist martyrs; it also blatantly erases the memory of the victims of the Holocaust. The former police station now houses the Chortkiv Institute of Business, but the rear of the building still serves as a prison. Here yet another memorial plaque has been put up, according to which "In the cells of this prison perished in 1941 more than 800 Ukrainian patriots at the hands of the Bolshevik hangmen." Once again, the fate of the many thousands of Jewish victims is not even alluded to.

Of all places it is at the Christian cemetery that we find a Communist monument. Declaring that "nothing is forgotten," this rather eclectic monument displays a bowing, bareheaded Soviet soldier, holding his helmet in his hand and seemingly contemplating the sacrifice of the war. At his feet is a Soviet star and on either side are the numerals 1941 and 1945, the years of the Great Patriotic War, which conveniently erase the Soviet occupation of Galicia in 1939–41 in alliance with Nazi Germany. Here too fresh wreaths of flowers are deposited. But along the same black brick wall that forms the original memorial a new post-Soviet cross has been erected to commemorate the victims of the famine of 1932–33, instigated, as every Ukrainian schoolchild knows, by the Kremlin. And, so as to add yet another dimension to this "competitions of victims," not far from this complex stands a Dominican memorial crypt, inscribed in Polish, to commemorate the "Fathers and Brothers slaughtered on July 2, 1941," of whom four, aged 31–84, were "murdered in the cloister," and another four, aged 31–46, were "murdered on the banks of the Seret." It is not clear whether these men were victims of the NKVD just before the Soviets withdrew, of Ukrainian nationalists rioting as the Germans were marching in, or of the Germans. But undoubtedly this memorial too could have only been put up after the fall of the Communist regime. It also highlights the fact that an entire other group of victims, which happens to have been by far the largest, has no commemorative mention anywhere in a town otherwise distinguished by its remembrances of past atrocities, martyrdom, and heroism.

For it is through this very same Christian cemetery that one can enter the old Jewish cemetery of Chortkiv. We walk across an overgrown field of grass with wild flowers swaying in the breeze, passing by old and new crosses and tombs, and can barely distinguish a concrete gateway, half covered with bushes, its doors ajar, inscribed with the Hebrew words "cemetery" and the Jewish dates equivalent to 1914–25. This is all that is left of the Jewish cemetery built to accommodate thousands of victims of the epidemics that raged in the area during World War I and took the lives of both residents and refugees evicted from surrounding villages in the course of the fighting. This was also the site of mass executions by the Nazis and, according to some photos and documents, where mass graves were located and several rows of tombstones survived the Nazi occupation.

But the gate leads nowhere, for on the other side is an impassable bush, in which only remnants of a few smashed or fallen tombstones can be glimpsed. The cemetery has vanished, swallowed by the lush vegetation of the region, abandoned by its owners, deprived of its tombstones by thieves and robbers. The "new" Jewish cemetery lies outside Chortkiv, on a hill overlooking the town and the beautiful rolling fields that surround it, by the banks of the Seret. It too is overgrown and neglected, but many of the stones, some dating back to the nineteenth century and others put up only after World War II—apparently by family members no longer living in town who wanted to be buried next to their loved ones—are still intact. Yet no

FIGURE 36. Chortkiv Hasidic Synagogue, 2004.

memorial stone has been put up on this remote site, which can be accessed only by crossing the fields and with some knowledge of the local geography.[108]

Two majestic synagogues still remain in Chortkiv, although at least one of them seems doomed to destruction. The famous

[108] There were in fact three Jewish cemeteries in Chortkiv. The ancient cemetery dates back to the early seventeenth century, but it was almost entirely destroyed by the Nazis and its tombstones were used to pave the city prison's courtyard and the town's sidewalks. See Austri-Dunn, *Memorial Book of Czortkow*, 160–65, and Tzvi Cohen, "Cemeteries in Chortkov," trans. Sara Mages, http://www.jewishgen.org/Yizkor/chortkov/cho156.html#Page160 (accessed December 3, 2006). See further in *RIS – Religious Information Service of Ukraine*, June 22, 2005 (http://www.risu.org.ua/eng/news/article;5804/ [accessed December 3, 2006]), according to which the Chortkiv city hospital dug up the ancient Jewish cemetery adjacent to it in order to use it as a

Hasidic synagogue, or the "Rabbi's Kloiz," built in the late nineteenth and early twentieth centuries, is now in a state of growing disrepair. While the structure is still sound, the paint and even the plaster are peeling off the exterior. The interior of the building has been altered and seems to be serving as a training center for youth; some of the space is taken up by agricultural machinery. Nothing indicates this eclectic edifice's original identity. Instead, a plaque attached to the wall by the main entrance triumphantly displays the first stanza and chorus of the Ukrainian national anthem:

> Ukraine's glory has not perished, nor her freedom
> Upon us, fellow compatriots, fate shall smile once more.
> Our enemies will vanish, like dew in the morning sun,
> And we too shall rule, brothers, in a free land of our own.
>
> We'll lay down our souls and bodies to attain our freedom,
> And we'll show that we, brothers, are of the Cossack nation.[109]

---

garden, despite the fact that the cemetery is registered with the central government as historical property. The cemetery is surrounded by a fence with no gate, and its few remaining tombstones were put up again by the Jewish community in 1990. The cemetery is now owned by the municipality, and its boundaries have shrunk because much of its grounds have been handed over to the hospital.

[109] Translated by Ihor W. Slabicky. The anthem was finally approved only in 2003 after a lengthy debate. The text is based on a patriotic poem written in 1862 by Pavlo Chubynsky. The original poem read "Shche ne vmerla Ukraïna" (Ukraine has not yet perished), but this was seen as too pessimistic. See further on the debate and changes introduced to the text of the poem in "official Ukrainian National Anthem Finally Decided in 2003," http://pages.prodigy.net/l.hodges/anthem.htm (accessed December 3, 2006). The original first line was borrowed from the Polish national anthem, "Dąbrowski's Mazurka," also known as "Jeszcze Polska nie zginęła" (Poland has not yet perished), from the first line of the lyrics, written in 1797 by

FIGURE 37. Chortkiv Great Synagogue, 2004.

The Great Synagogue, built in 1771, is empty, bricked up and fenced in. Until a few years ago the synagogue could be freely approached. In June 2004, however, construction was proceeding right next to it, and one could approach the building only

---

Józef Wybicki, one of the organizers of general Jan Henryk Dąbrowski's Polish Army in Italy. The line refers to the partitions of Poland that destroyed it as an independent state by 1795. Poland adopted this song as its national anthem in 1927. See "Poland: 'Mazurek Dabrowskiego' (Dabrowski's Mazurka)," http://david.national-anthems.net/pl.htm (accessed December 3, 2006); "National Anthems of Poland," http://www.usc.edu/dept/polish_music/repertoi/dabrowski.html (accessed December 3, 2006). The Israeli National Anthem. "Ha-Tikvah," has also been influenced by the polish anthem.

by jumping a fence or by leaping over the foundations of a building that was going up on Hohol' (Gogol) Street, behind the synagogue. With the completion of the building there will be no access to this once handsome edifice. One can only assume that the synagogue will eventually be torn down.

Most recently, however, a new memorial to the murdered Jews of Chortkiv has been installed. It is not easy to find information on it, and the local or state authorities do not seem to have had anything to do with its erection. In July 2005 the Internet magazine *Human Rights in Ukraine* posted a report by Oleksandr Stepanenko, according to which on the twentieth of that month a memorial plaque was put up in the Black Forest next to the site where thousands of Jews had been shot and buried in mass graves. The opening ceremony was said to have included visitors from Israel, Poland, France, and the United States—apparently relatives of the victims. Stepanenko notes that many such mass graves, containing thousands of victims, are scattered in the region. He also reminds his readers that Jews constituted between a third and a half of the urban population of Galicia and Western Podolia for much of the previous four centuries. Mentioning some of the names of the great rabbis of Chortkiv, such as David-Moshe Fridman, and such well-known writers as Emil Franzos of Chortkiv and Shmuel Yosef Agnon of Buchach, he asks: "Who is guilty of these many thousands of deaths? Fascism? Nationalist and ideological narrow-mindedness? The emergence of the 'age of the masses' "? His conclusion: "Yesterday's extermination is perpetuated in today's oblivion." This is true. But Stepanenko is complicit in one aspect of this silence, which echoes all the more powerfully precisely because his is the only—and rather obscure—mention of this memorial and its context. For he neglects to remind his readers, however few they may be, that fellow Ukrainians, likely not a few of their own ancestors, participated in the mass murder of their Jewish neighbors.[110]

[110] Oleksandr Stepanenko, "Znovu zhe—Pro pravo ne buty zabutymy" [Again—About the Right Not to Be Forgotten], *Prava Ludyiy* 17 (July 5, 2005), http://www.khpg.org/index.php?id=1120579442&w=%F1%F2%E5%EF%E0 %ED%E5%ED%EA%EE (accessed December 3, 2006). Thanks to Sofia Grachova, who drew my attention to this posting. It must also be mentioned here that a few citizens of Chortkiv bravely helped their Jewish neighbors and thus saved their lives. Frida Gizler and another young Jewish woman were saved by Mrs. Uhrynska, a pole; Shushana Carmi, her two-year-old daughter, and her brother were hidden by the Ukrainian Anna Aksenczuk; David Sheviger, his wife, their daughter, his father, and six more Jews were hidden by the Polish couple Viktor Kotowicz and his wife—the latter even traveled to L'viv and brought the daughters of another Jew to the shelter. But these cases were rare. Gizler writes that had Uhrynska's "neighbors found out that she was hiding us, they would have notified the authorities. Many like them hunted and killed Jews with their own hands. In a time when non-Jews [*sic*] residents were robbing and killing Jews, almost daily, this wonderful woman sheltered Jews." Carmi writes of the "curious" side of her situation at Aksenczuk's home, since this "woman's son was second in command in the Ukrainian police. He used to visit his mother every week, not knowing about the Jews that she was hiding in her barn. The woman was sure that her son would never risk his life, or his status in the police department, because of a few Jews." As for Kotowicz, whose father was a hunchback coachman, and who worked himself as a porter, he seems to illustrate the fact that in Galicia Poles were generally more likely than Ukrainians to help Jews—since they too became a threatened minority—and that working people were often more altruistic than the more nationalistic-minded intelligentsia. See "Lights out of Darknessing," http://www.jewishgen.org/Yizkor/chortkov/cho347.html#Page347 (accessed December 3, 2006). For books by Karl Emil Franzos (1848–1904), who gave Chortkiv the literary name Barnow in his writings, see "Additional Readings."

Zolotyi Potik / Potok Złoty / Zolotoy Potok / Potek Zolti

Figure 38. Jewish cemetery in Zolotyi Potik, 2004.

Heading southwest from Chortkiv we reach Zolotyi Potik, about 13 miles southwest of Buchach and 46 miles southwest of Ternopil'.[111] Declared a private city belonging to the noble Polish Potocki family in 1570, the town was fortified and given a

[111] Based mainly on *Pinkas Hakehillot*, 415–16. See also "Potok Złoty," http://www.shtetlinks.jewishgen.org/Suchostaw/sl_potokzloty.htm (accessed December 3, 2006); Stanisław Jankowski, *Potok Złoty: Jaki w pamięci pozostał* (Opole: Wabienice, 1996).

124

Dominican monastery in the early seventeenth century. As of 1635 we know of a Jewish community in Zolotyi Potik. By the beginning of the twentieth century there were about a thousand Jews in the town, comprising close to a third of the population. The town was heavily damaged in World War I, and by the early 1920s its population stood at just over 3,000 people, of whom 895 were Jews. During the German occupation of the region in World War II, Zolotyi Potik was ruled by the Ukrainian militia, which looted and oppressed the Jewish population. In September or October 1942 the Jews were deported to Buchach and perished there with much of the rest of that town's population (see the next section).

In June 2004 the Jewish cemetery of Zolotyi Potik was serving, as it has for many decades, as a meadow for the local goats. Some of its extraordinary tombstones, dating back several centuries and decorated with intricate carvings, were still standing. Others were piled up and ready to be carted off somewhere. Their future use was unknown. But it was not difficult to determine how such tombstones had been used in the past. The staircase to the only habitable part of the once grand but now ruined Potocki palace was supported by Jewish gravestones, as were the steps and banister leading to the formerly elegant prewar villa, serving now in its much shabbier state as a "Municipal Veterans' Clinic." A displaced tombstone, possibly fallen off a cart as it was being carried away from the cemetery and never picked up, was lying in the grove by the clinic. The inscription read: "The important virgin, Miss Leah, daughter of Israel, may her soul be gathered in the bundle of life."

Since my mother was born in Zolotyi Potik in 1924, I asked an old lady at the cemetery whether she remembered the Szimer family. She smiled, revealing her single gold tooth, and nodded vigorously. But she had nothing else to add and had obviously merely wanted to please a visiting foreigner. Still,

FIGURE 39. Banister and staircase made of Jewish gravestones, Zolotyi Potik, 2004.

when visiting the manor house next to the palace's romantic ruin, I tried to imagine what things might have looked like eighty years earlier. My maternal great-grandfather had served as estate manager for the Potockis in Zolotyi Potik, and for all I knew it was precisely in that courtyard that my mother had spent the first year of her life, before the family moved to Buchach in 1925. I am not a believer in ghosts or miracles. But had it not been for the upheavals of the intervening decades, I too might have called this patch of dirt my home.

Buchach / Buczacz / Butschatsch / Bitshutsh

FIGURE 40. The Great Synagogue and Beit Hamidrash, Buchach, 1922 (photo credit: Beth Hatefutsoth, Photo Archive, Tel Aviv).

WE ARE DRIVING along the Strypa Valley on a winding dirt road. This, my Ukrainian assistant says, must be the same path that my great-grandfather traveled by wagon to buy or sell goods in Buchach. It is a quiet and peaceful afternoon. Only the sound of the car's wheels rolling on the gravel disturbs the silence. The Strypa keeps flowing slowly to the Dnister, just as it did all those decades ago.[112]

---

[112] I am currently writing a history of Buchach. The bibliography is too vast to be covered here. For references see Omer Bartov, "Seeking the Roots of

Buchach was established in the fourteenth century and had a Jewish population at least since 1500. The city was heavily damaged in the Cossack and Turkish wars of the seventeenth century but subsequently recovered. It was known for its massive synagogue (1728) and its elegant town hall (1751), as well as for its churches, Basilian monastery, the remnants of its Renaissance fortress, and its remarkable location, perched on hills rising above the winding Strypa River. On the eve of World War I the town numbered over 14,000 inhabitants, more than half of whom were Jews, the rest being either Poles or Ukrainians. Well over half the houses in Buchach were either destroyed or seriously damaged during the fighting and the city's population was halved. But in the interwar period Buchach gradually recovered. It is estimated that there were some 10,000 Jews in the town at the outbreak of World War II.

The Germans occupied Buchach in early July 1941 and a few weeks later they murdered several hundred "intellectuals" on

---

Modern Genocide: On the Macro- and Microhistory of Mass Murder," in *The Specter of Genocide: Mass Murder in Historical Perspective*, ed. Robert Gellately and Ben Kiernan (Cambridge: Cambridge University Press, 2003), 75–96; Bartov, "Les relations interethniques à Buczacz." See further in *Pinkas Hakehillot*, 83–89; Yisrael Kohen, ed., *The Book of Buczacz* (Tel Aviv: Am Oved, 1956, in Hebrew), http://yizkor.nypl.org/index.php?id=1854 (accessed December 3, 2006), English translation, http://www.jewishgen.org/Yizkor/buchach/buchach.html (accessed December 3, 2006). Further information and sources at "Dotokzłoty http://www.shtetlinks.jewishgen.org/Suchostaw/sl_buczacz.htm (accessed December 3, 2006). For memoirs from Buchach and the nearby towns of Podhajce and Tluste, as well as literary accounts, see "Additional Readings." For biographies of the town's more famous sons, see Dan Laor, *S. Y. Agnon: A Biography* (Tel Aviv: Schocken, 1998, in Hebrew); Hella Pick, *Simon Wiesenthal: A Life in Search of Justice* (London: Weidenfeld & Nicolson, 1996); Samuel Kassow, "A Stone Under History's Wheel: The Story of Emanuel Ringelblum and the *Oneg Shabes* Archive," http://yiddishbookcenter.org/pdf/pt/43/PT43ringelblum.pdf (accessed December 3, 2006).

nearby Fedir (Fedor) Hill. The first massive *Aktion* took place in October 1942. About 1,600 Jews were transported to Bełżec and another 200 were shot on the spot by the Germans and their Ukrainian collaborators. In November another 2,500 were taken to Bełżec, and about 250 were hunted down and shot with the assistance of some of the local population. In late 1942 a ghetto was established, in which Jews from nearby towns were also concentrated. In February 1942 approximately 2,000 Jews were shot and buried in mass graves on Fedir Hill. The killings continued throughout the spring, costing the lives of 3,000 people. In June 1943 the last remnants of the community were shot at the Jewish cemetery along with those who worked in the labor camp in town.

Remarkably, when the city was liberated in March 1944, about 800 Jews came out of hiding, an indication that despite the collaboration of local gentiles, many also assisted the Jews. However, the Germans counterattacked and seized the town again shortly thereafter, subsequently murdering most of the survivors. By the time the Red Army finally drove the Germans out in July, only 100 Jews were still alive in the area. During the last months of the war the substantial Polish population of the entire region was also subjected to a massive campaign of ethnic cleansing, which ultimately terminated the presence of Polish life and culture in Galicia along with the extermination of the Jews.

Present-day Buchach, like all other towns in Western Ukraine, is almost entirely ethnically homogeneous. Its memory of the past parallels its ethnic and religious identity. While a few people still remember the events of the war and even some of the specific victims, there is no collective memory of either the presence or the elimination of non-Ukrainians. Still, as in Chortkiv, the Polish past, or at least its Christian faith, is treated more respectfully: the Roman Catholic church has been beautifully restored and its priest, Father Ludwik, who was born in Buchach in 1917 and fled from it in 1939, has been living there since he returned in 1995. But visitors to Buchach will not find any official indication of this city's rich Jewish past. The Great Synagogue, which can still be seen standing in a German aerial photograph taken in April 1944, is no more. There is no indication in town of where it once stood, although its location can be established from old photographs. The site now serves as an open market.

For a long time it was difficult to find out what had become of the massive, thick-walled Groyse Shul (Great Synagogue). But in March 2006 the local resident Oresta Synen'ka, whose family moved to the city in 1945, related that her father had worked there as the foreman of a building brigade until 1950. According to her, a whole block of houses had been heavily damaged—apparently in the last bout of fighting over the city in the late spring and summer of 1944—and the workers had to decide which houses to repair and which to tear down. "There was no sense in repairing the synagogue," she said, "so they demolished it. It was done by 1950."[113]

The study house (Beit Hamidrash) adjacent to the synagogue stood near the center of town until 2001. That year it was torn down to make room for a shopping center, despite the protests of some Israeli tourists who happened to have been there at the time and took photographs of the bulldozer as it demolished the structure. The Jewish cemetery on Bashty Hill overlooking the town (on the opposite side of Fedir Hill) still contains some tombstones, including that of the writer Agnon's father, Shalom Mordechai Chachkes. These tombstones were

---

[113] Interview with Oresta Synen'ka and her husband Ivan Synen'kyi conducted by Sofia Grachova and Andriy Pavlyashuk on March 2, 2006, in Buchach.

FIGURE 41. Jewish cemetery in Buchach, 2003.

recently cleaned up and photographed by the retired MIT professor Thomas Weiss and his sons, some of whose family originally came from Buchach. Another, largely overgrown part of the cemetery, located on the slope leading down to the city, contains stones dating back to 1587.[114]

In order to find the cemetery one needs some prior knowledge of the town or a local guide, since no signs have been put up directing visitors to this site where thousands of Jews were shot. A memorial was put up there by the few survivors immediately after the war, but it disappeared many years ago, no one

---

[114] Nosonovsky, *Hebrew Epitaphs and Inscriptions*, 25. For a wealth of information and photos, see "Buczacz," http://www.shtetlinks.jewishgen.org/Suchostaw/sl_buczacz.htm (accessed December 3, 2006).

knows where. The empty field next to the cemetery, which the Jews used to call the "Chazerplatz" because it had served as an open market for selling swine, was used by the Germans to assemble Jews before they were taken either for execution at the cemetery or to the train station for the transport to Bełżec. Again no sign has been put up to indicate this.

Similarly, the handsome gymnasium, built during the rule of the Habsburg Empire in the late nineteenth century, bears no commemorative plaque to its numerous Jewish and Polish students, many of whom ended up being deported by the Soviets or murdered by the Germans and Ukrainian collaborators and nationalists. Conversely, a commemorative plaque placed inside the school is said to be dedicated to the Ukrainian students arrested by the Soviet authorities there.[115] Indeed, as another plaque installed by the school gate indicates, the gymnasium is now named after Volodymyr Hnatiuk, an important figure in the revival of Ukrainian culture, who was born in Buchach County in 1871 and worked closely with the poet Ivan Franko. Hnatiuk eventually became general secretary of the Shevchenko Scientific Society in L'viv and served as an active member of the Prosvita Society, also in L'viv.[116] Although the recently deceased Simon Wiesenthal, later internationally known as the "Nazi hunter," was born in Buchach and attended the gymnasium in the 1920s, no mention is made of him there.[117]

The forested Fedir Hill contains mass graves of many thousands of the town's former Jewish residents. Here too, however,

[115] This is according to Petro Pasichnyk (born in 1923), interviewed by Sofia Grachova and Andriy Pavlyashuk on March 3, 2006, in Buchach. I have not been able to enter the gymnasium to verify this information.

[116] See: "Volodymyr Hnatiuk," *Lviv Best Portal*, http://www.lvivbest.com/Sections+index-req-viewarticle-artid-140-page-1.html (accessed December 3, 2006).

[117] Pick, *Simon Wiesenthal*, 42–43.

even if one knew about these events, it would be impossible to find the site of the graves, let alone the lone memorial standing there, without the help of a local guide. The memorial is a simple tombstone-sized edifice that actually commemorates the victims of the "registration *Aktion*," the first mass execution of the Jewish "intelligentsia." The inscription, written only in Ukrainian, reads simply: "Here rest 450 people slain by the German executioners on August 27, 1941."[118] While a Star of David is carved on the stone, the written text lacks any identification of the victims' identity. As reported in June 2004 by Roman Antoshkiv, a retired employee of the city's administration, for most of the Communist period the stone lay broken into two parts on the forest floor. It was put up again in the 1990s on the initiative of Antoshkiv and the Jewish principal of the agricultural school on Fedir Hill, who provided cement and a tractor for this purpose.[119]

There is one impressive memorial on Fedir Hill—a large cross planted on a round mound of earth that can be seen from afar—but it is dedicated to the UPA freedom fighters who had first helped the Germans murder the Jews and then resisted the reoccupation of the region by the Red Army. At the bottom of the cross is a plaque with the rhymed verse: "Glorious heroes who have fallen [in the struggle] for freedom / holy knights, hear this

[118] Estimates of the actual number of people murdered in this first mass shooting range between 350 and 700.

[119] I interviewed Roman Antoshkiv in Buchach on June 21, 2004. Antoshkiv was born and raised in the 1930s in a nearby village. He related that his mother worked for the Jews and, as he put it, thanks to that experience she could distinguish between good Jews and bad Jews. He recalled the day on which the Jews of the village were assembled by the Germans and led away, presumably to Buchach. Antoshkiv was mentioned in the local press around the time of the interview as one of the citizens who donated money to the construction of the Bandera monument (see more later in the book).

in your graves / We swear here, by your grave, to preserve the freedom of Ukraine." This post-independence memorial stands in competition with an older monument, erected during the Soviet regime, which is located elsewhere on the same hill. Featuring an oversized Red Army soldier, the monument is simply inscribed with the words "Eternal Memory to the Fallen Heroes," and the dates 1941–45, clearly indicating that it is about the Great Patriotic War of the Soviet Union against Nazi Germany and bears no link to, and indeed refutes the legitimacy of, the Ukrainian struggle against the Soviets. The cross attached to the side of the monument was obviously added only after 1991.

Buchach also now contains a museum for the UPA, situated in the former offices of the NKVD and put together in the early 1990s by the same Oresta Synen'ka quoted above, who works there voluntarily as part of her self-appointed task of preserving the memory of Ukraine's local freedom fighters and victims of the NKVD, one of whom was her husband, Ivan Synen'kyi.[120]

---

[120] See n. 113, in this section. I am thankful to Sofia Grachova for photographing the memorials and the museum, translating the texts, and conducting the interviews. It is unlikely that those interviewed would have expressed themselves in the same manner had I been present; indeed, they would have most probably refused to be interviewed in the first place. Oresta Synen'ka noted in her interview that "a few Poles came back" to Buchach. Commenting on the 89-year-old Roman Catholic Father Ludwik, she said: "They have an old priest. But we keep them in their place." She also related that on Fedir Hill the bones of the murdered Jews could still be seen, presumably because of the shallow graves. She remarked: "I asked the mayor, as well as the principal of the college [presumably the agricultural school situated on the hill] many times: take a few fellows from the college and make them scatter some earth over the grave. There are people lying about there, never mind who they were." Ivan Synen'kyi was born in Buchach in 1925 and served as a member of UPA, probably as of 1944, taking photographs of Soviet agents, which would then be delivered to the UPA units in the forest. He was arrested on May 14, 1946, and spent ten years in Soviet camps. See also "The testimony of Ivan Iosypovych Synen'kyi," recorded for the *Poshuk Archive*, October 29, 2004.

FIGURE 42. UPA museum in Buchach, 2006 (photo credit: Sofia Grachova).

Finally, another monument has been erected in the yard of St. Nicholas Greek Catholic Church, situated on a hill overlooking the town center. It is a simple wooden cross commemorating the sixtieth anniversary of the Ukrainian famine of 1933. When I visited the site in March 2003, there was a bouquet of fresh flowers at the foot of the cross.

The only site in town where a former Jewish presence is publicly acknowledged is the humble museum in the main square. Here several glass cases containing books by Agnon, mostly donated by visiting Israeli tourists in 2001, make a somewhat ghostly appearance, in that no context is provided for the presence of this yarmulke-wearing, Hebrew-language author in

what is otherwise an almost purely Ukrainian town. Nevertheless, the belated revelation of this former resident's celebrity
stimulated the municipality to rename the street on which he
lived at the beginning of the twentieth century. An elaborate
marble plaque that was put up at 5 Agnon Street in 2003 to
commemorate the author's residence—now a rather derelict
tenement—was stolen soon thereafter. It was replaced by a
simpler sign in a wooden frame, which reads: "In this house
lived in 1888–1907 the writer, Nobel Prize laureate (1966)
Shmuel Yosef Agnon (Chachkes), July 17, 1888—February 17,
1970." Written only in Ukrainian, the plaque makes no mention of the author's Jewish identity or the language in which
he wrote. Nor did this modest commemorative effort have
any effect on the demolition of the study house which features so prominently in Agnon's voluminous writings on his
hometown.[121]

Every other opportunity to commemorate Jewish life and
death in Buchach has been missed. No plaque has been attached
to the local police station and jail, though parts of it have been
renovated, to indicate that it served to hold many of those who
were subsequently led up the path to be shot on Fedir Hill, or
were transported to the larger Gestapo prison in Chortkiv. No
plaque has been put up at the Christian cemetery to commemorate the heroism of the undertaker Manko Szwierszczak, who
hid four Jews for almost two years in a crypt and later under his

---

[121] Agnon's *A Guest for the Night* contains retrospectively tragic sections
in which the author, who visited Buchach in 1930, looks out of the windows
of the study house to Fedir Hill, where the community would be murdered a
few years later, and reminisces about family picnics and lovers' rendezvous
there before World War I. Agnon's posthumous book, *The Whole City*, is a
vast collection of tales, legends, and historical accounts about Jewish life in
Buchach, much of it centered around its many synagogues. See "Additional
Readings."

house.[122] The train station, from which some 5,000 Jews were sent to Bełżec, carries no sign indicating this event. The railroad tunnel, blown up by the retreating Soviets in 1941, rebuilt by Jewish slave labor under the Nazis, and still used by freight trains to this day, bears no plaque identifying these workers, most of whom eventually perished. The site of the Jewish hospital, the most modern in the region before World War II, is now an empty lot without any mark of its past glory or the ghastly manner in which its Jewish patients were murdered by the Germans.

Recently, however, Buchach too has been undergoing a memory renaissance. The town is currently in the process of constructing a monument for Stepan Bandera on a hill that overlooks Buchach from the other bank of the Strypa. The funds for this edifice were collected by public subscription among the citizens of the town, despite its depressed economy. This is part of a larger nationalist undertaking in Buchach, which is currently catching up with the many other towns in the region that have already constructed nationalist monuments and museums. In January 2006 the town celebrated the ninety-seventh anniversary of Bandera's birth with solemn patriotic speeches and a performance by the women's choir.[123]

---

[122] Mordecai Paldiel, *The Path of the Righteous: Gentile Rescuers of Jews during the Holocaust* (Hoboken, N.J.: Ktav, 1992), 191–93.

[123] See "Buchach: Novyny Mista" [Buchach: New city], http://www.buchachnews.iatp.org.ua/foto/displayimage.php?album=2&pos=46 (accessed December 3, 2006); "Horyachye Novosti" [Hot News], http://buchach.com.ua/?mhnews_id=206&mhnews_newsid=7310&mhnews_page=1 (accessed December 3 , 2006). Among the speakers was the director of the Bandera Memorial (Society), Oresta Synen'ka, mentioned in this section. The speeches are said to been "beautiful and sincere . . . full of heartfelt feelings, reflections on the figure of Stepan Bandera in the history of our Fatherland and the region, and his enormous role in the formation of Ukrainian self-consciousness, national spirit, and the striving for freedom and liberty." This information was available at "Buchach," http://buchach.info, but is no longer posted there.

The event took place at a building that had previously served the Sokół (Falcon), the Polish gymnastics and cultural association, but had been made available before the war also for Jewish and Ukrainian groups. But the plaque on this elegant structure, built in 1905, as well as the city's Internet announcement of the event, blandly describes the building it as the "District Culture House," making no reference to its past role in bringing together the different groups that had once inhabited the city.

Conversely, in May 2005 a concrete base for a monument was built at the site of the Jewish cemetery. Any such attempt to commemorate the fate of the Jews in Buchach seems to cause consternation. One local resident complained that the foreign Jews who asked Mayor Overko to build the base never paid him. They also offered to pay for a fence around the mass graves on Fedir Hill, but this informant claimed that the money was insufficient and that in any case people would steal the fence for the metal.[124] For now the future of this monument, meant to replace the postwar edifice that vanished shortly after it was erected, remains unclear. Meanwhile tombstones are still being carted away to serve other, more immediate needs, and hens roam the area, pecking at the garbage that people dump on the unfenced grounds of the cemetery.[125] Other, more future-oriented work is being carried out in Buchach. Until recently there was no hotel in the town save for a truckers' bed and breakfast hardly recommended to foreigners. Now the hotel that had once belonged to the Jewish Anderman family before the war is being renovated, and another hotel has recently opened. For the first time in almost seventy years Buchach will

[124] Interview with Mykola Kozak conducted in Buchach by Sofia Grachova on March 2, 2006.

[125] For photos of tombstones by Tom Weiss and his sons, see "Index of Gravestones in Jewish Cemetery in Buchach," http://www.shtetlinks.jewishgen.org/Suchostav/Buchach/BuchCemIndex.html (accessed December 3, 2006).

FIGURE 43. Base for monument at Jewish cemetery, Buchach, 2006 (photo credit: Sofia Grachova).

be able to accommodate tourists, although it may still be hesitant about revealing to them the secrets of its past.

My maternal grandfather received a certificate of immigration to Palestine in March 1935. My mother, her two brothers, and their parents, landed at the port of Haifa in December that year. From a comfortable bourgeois existence they were reduced to the status of blue-collar workers. My grandmother, who had been educated at a gymnasium in Prague when the family fled the Russians in World War I and spoke fluent German as well as Yiddish, Hebrew, Polish, and Ukrainian, worked for years in an orange-packing facility and cleaned the houses of richer neighbors on the Sabbath. My grandfather worked as

FIGURE 44. City Hall with Shevchenko monument, Buchach, 2004.

a laborer until he was felled by a heart attack. My mother was the first in her family to have a college degree. But the rest of the extended family (with the exception of one uncle who left in 1935 for South America) disappeared without a trace. No one knows how they were murdered or where their bodies lie. I am the only member of my family to have returned to Buchach. By then my mother had passed away. I am glad that we never accomplished our plan to go there together. She had fond memories of her childhood there and took them to her grave without seeing the merciless erasure of the postwar years.

As I was leaving Buchach in June 2004, the sky cleared and the sun lit the main square and the still handsome, though dilapidated, town hall, with a soft afternoon glow. The massive stone statue of Ukraine's national poet, Taras Shevchenko, looked out toward the bridge over the Strypa, the Basilian Monastery, and Fedir Hill in the distance. This was the path the Jews of the city had followed on their way to execution in public view of all other residents. I was standing more or less where the synagogue had once stood, as a funeral procession wound its way down from the monastery to the marketplace. A coffin was being carried on the back of a truck. In front of the procession marched two men carrying flags: the blue and yellow national flag of Ukraine, and the black and red flag of UPA. Ukrainian Buchach had come into its own.

Monastyrys'ka / Monasterzyska / Monastrishtz / Monastyrisce

FIGURE 45. Gallery of Ukrainian heroes, Monastyrys'ka, 2004.

TRAVELING some ten miles northwest of Buchach, we come to Monastyrys'ka.[126] Founded as a private town in the mid-sixteenth century, the city is known to have had a Jewish population since 1625. By the eve of World War I the town's 2,000

[126] This account is based primarily on *Pinkas Hakehillot*, 309–13. See also Meir Segal, ed., *Monasterzyska: A Memorial Book* (Tel Aviv: Monasterzyska Association in Israel, 1974); "Monasterzyska," http://www.shtetlinks.jewishgen.org/ Suchostaw/sl_monasterzyska.htm (accessed December 3, 2006). See also Zbigniew Żyromski, *Miasto Kresowe: Monasterzyska wczoraj i dziś* (Wrocław: Towarzystwo

Jewish inhabitants constituted half of the total population. Monastyrys'ka had a large tobacco factory that employed hundreds of workers, as well as a toy factory and other enterprises. Conquered twice by the Russian army in World War I and severely damaged in the fighting, the town was also subjected to widespread violence and looting under the ephemeral Ukrainian republic and during the Russo-Polish War, in which the bands of the nationalist leader Symon Petliura robbed, murdered, and raped members of the Jewish community. By the early 1920s the population of the city had been halved, and even in the early 1930s there were less than 1,500 Jewish residents in Monastyrys'ka. Following the outbreak of World War II the town absorbed a large number of Jewish refugees from German-occupied Poland, many of whom were employed in the tobacco factory during the two years of Soviet rule.

The Germans occupied the town in early July 1941 and along with Ukrainian policemen proceeded to rob, humiliate, and murder the town's Jews and refugees from neighboring villages who fled into Monastyrys'ka. In October 1942 the Germans conducted a first massive *Aktion*, in which some 800 people were sent to Bełżec, several scores were shot on the spot, and a group of healthy young men was sent to the Yaniv (Janowska) concentration camp in L'viv. Soon thereafter the town was declared *Judenrein* and all the surviving Jews moved to Buchach. The new Jewish cemetery was the site of mass killings of Jews found hiding or among the partisans in the forests. Only twenty Jews survived the war, of whom ten had fled to the Soviet

---

Miłośników Lwowa i Kresów Południowo-Wschodnich Oddział Buczacz, 2003), a lament of Polish Monasterzyska that also mentions the life and death of the Jewish population but provides only one photograph of the town's synagogue out of a total of 204 depicting its Polish and Catholic past. Ibid., 106, photo 158.

Union. One local resident is known to have hidden a Jewish family of four who consequently survived the Holocaust. Following the Soviet reoccupation of Monastyrys'ka, both Jewish cemeteries were made into public gardens, while the synagogue was converted into a grain-storage facility.

On a rainy afternoon in June 2004, Monastyrys'ka looked as if it was still in the process of recovery from decades of Soviet neglect and local amnesia. The town's more handsome houses were in a state of disrepair. Some former stately structures were being slowly restored. The old tobacco factory did not show any signs of modernization. Opposite it, however, the symbols of Ukrainian nationalism had been erected. A bronze statue of Taras Shevchenko now overlooks a row of busts representing Ukrainian national history: Prince Volodymyr Velykyi (the Great) who Christianized Kievan Rus' in the tenth century; Prince Yaroslav Mudryi (the Wise) of the eleventh century; Prince Dmytro Vyshnevets'kyi, a sixteenth-century Cossack hetman; the seventeenth-century Cossack hetman Petro Sahaidachnyi; Bohdan Khmel'nyts'kyi, the seventeenth-century unifier of Ukraine and scourge of the Jews; Ivan Mazepa, the last ruler of the Cossack state in the late seventeenth and early eighteenth centuries; the national historian Mykhailo Hrushevskyi, active at the turn of the previous century; and, finally, the early twentieth-century nationalist leader Petliura, also remembered for the pogroms perpetrated by his men on innumerable Jewish communities in the wake of World War I.[127]

The portrait gallery of Ukrainian national heroes stands with its back to the remains of Monastyrys'ka's synagogue. Built at

---

[127] For a balanced evaluation of Petliura's role in the pogroms, see Henry Abramson, *A Prayer for the Government: Ukrainians and Jews in Revolutionary Times, 1917–1920* (Cambridge, Mass.: Harvard University Press, 1999), esp. 109–140; for a more accusatory view, see Saul S. Friedman, *Pogromchik: The Assassination of Simon Petlura* (New York: Hart Publishing Company, 1976).

FIGURE 46. Synagogue in Monastyrys'ka, 2004.

the turn of the century, the building now serves as a furniture store. While the interior of the synagogue was destroyed by the Jews under German orders during the occupation, the structure itself is still solid, though derelict. It is surrounded by the usual piles of garbage. When I visited the site, a fire was burning in front of the building, either in order to warm the owner crouching next to it, or to burn some of the trash. Chickens were pecking at the ground. As the rain intensified we walked into the building, only to find a display of cheap and ungainly Soviet-era furniture that no one seemed in a particular hurry to buy. It was time to get out of town.

Ternopil' / Tarnopol / Ternopol

FIGURE 47. Allegory of Ukrainian independence, Ternopil' museum, 2004.

We head northeast to Ternopil' on the Seret River, capital of the Ternopil' Oblast', located some 80 miles east of L'viv. With a population of 221,300 in 2004, this is one of the three main cities of Eastern Galicia.[128] I had worked in the Ternopil' state archives in March 2003 and then visited the city again in June 2004. It is an elegant town that proudly displays some elements of its past glory, mostly restored since the fall of

---

[128] *Wikipedia*, S.V. "Ternopil," http://en.wikipedia.org/wiki/Ternopil (accessed December 3, 2006).

Communism. But other reminders of the past have vanished without a trace.

Indeed, Ternopil' seems especially anxious about revealing certain aspects of its history. The director of the archives, Mr. Bohdan Vasyl'ovych Khavarivs'kyi, appeared somewhat worried about my activities there and personally inspected, stamped, and signed every document I was allowed to photocopy. These worries seemed to focus on two issues. First, that I might be seeking information on stolen Jewish property that could lead to demands for compensation (a worry also expressed by such seemingly uninvolved residents as the cab driver who inquired what a foreigner was going to look for in the archives). And second, that I would discover documents about Ukrainian collaboration with the Nazis. In fact, I did find a catalogue reference to a dossier by the postwar Soviet authorities in Buchach, the town I am researching, which promised to provide some useful information on the murder of the Jews. But for several years it remained impossible to gain access to this dossier, which was described invariably as either secret or harmful to Ukraine's image. Only very recently have I managed to obtain a copy of this important dossier, which contains documents on the extermination of the Jews by the Nazis, the deportation of Polish inhabitants, and the liquidation of UPA members by the Soviets.[129]

This past is, of course, hardly inaccessible. But as long as it is denied or hidden away in locked drawers, it casts a dark shadow on the present. It was consistent with this anxiety about past secrets being revealed that in March 2003 one of the city's main newspapers, the right-wing *Ne zdamos'!* (We Will Not

---

[129] For this I wish to thank my research assistant, Dr. Frank Grelka. See State Archives of the Ternopil' Region, fond R-279, opys 1, sprava 1; fond R-274, opys 1, sprava 123; fond P-1, opys 1, sprava 608; fond P-69, opys 1, sprava 1–2, 8, 17, 19, 31, 35–37, 38–40, 47.

Surrender!), published a front-page article by its editor, Yaroslav Demydas', entitled "Jewish Pogrom."[130] Arguing that the long history of oppression and murder of the Ukrainians by the Jews had culminated in the corrupt and criminal administration of Leonid Kuchma in Kyiv—detested in Western Ukraine and widely believed to be under Jewish influence—the article went on to "uncover" what it claimed to be the hidden truths of Ukraine's past.[131]

It may be instructive to cite some of the more blatantly anti-Semitic statements made in this widely available Ternopil' newspaper in order to illustrate the extent to which obfuscation, lies, and ignorance still prevail in this region. Thus Demydas' notes that in the past, presumably under the Communists,

> We were taught internationalism and a respectful attitude toward other peoples. In truth, we were encouraged to look at our own people with contempt. Those who fought for Ukraine were labeled "bandits." On the suffering of Ukrainians not a word was said, because in this falsified history it was the Jews who suffered most. For this other peoples had to bow down to them, to be in their debt, to be afraid of them.

[130] Yaroslav Demydas', "Zhydivs'kyi Pohrom," *Ne zdamos'*, no. 3 (March 2003), 1, 7. The article appeared under the heading "Editor's column" and can thus be described as an editorial. For the contested implications of using the term *zhyd* in Western Ukraine, see n. 46 in this section.

[131] Leonid Kuchma was president of Ukraine in 1994–2005. His presidency ended with the Orange Revolution, which brought Viktor Yushchenko to power with massive support from Western Ukraine. As this is being written, however, Viktor Yanukovych, leader of the Party of the Regions and prime minister of Ukraine in 2002–04 under Kuchma, with whom he is closely associated, who lost the presidential elections to Yushchenko in 2004, has led his party to victory in the parliamentary elections of March 2006, receiving 32 percent of the vote as opposed to Yushchenko's bloc, Our Ukraine, whose party received 14 percent, and Yulya Timoshenko's party's 22 percent. Consequently, on August 3, 2006, Yanukovych was appointed prime minister by President Yushchenko.

Indeed, from the author's point of view,

how was it possible not to be afraid of them when every high-ranking Soviet official either was a Jew himself or had a Jewish wife and when they all had the ear of Stalin's Gestapo [the NKVD], which was swarming with Jews . . . [?] By now everyone understands that this Soviet regime was planned and established by Jewish magnates and that Jews held all the key positions.

The consequences of this Jewish takeover were disastrous. For the Jews soon

occupied executive positions in the people's commissariats, swam in blood at secret-police headquarters, and wielded axes, crowbars, bayonets, and pistols in the "slaughter yards" and "slaughter cells." They surrounded Ukraine with a cordon of commissars and set about butchering and pillaging. They snatched the last crust of bread from children and the last hope from their elders. Those who were still living were driven to graves and buried alive. All in the name of the "radiant future." Jews also . . . enriched themselves and lived in luxury by taking away from Ukrainians their last family relics in exchange for a handful of groats or a couple of potatoes. They took away all the gold Ukrainians had, enriching themselves on blood and death.

Nor was this merely a matter of individual greed but a reflection of national essence and ideological drive:

For this is the Zionist profession: to act as parasites, to exploit, and to rob. These beasts in human form hurled seven million Ukrainians into their graves [an allusion to Stalin's state-directed famine of 1932–33] and buried Ukraine's future. The Zionists wanted to rule the world and intended to make our abundant land into a bridgehead for their conquests. . . . Flowering orchards and cottages were turned into a desert, and weeds ravaged the once fertile black earth. "A bit of bread!" a child would plead and then fall dead. Yes, Jewish commissars became infamous for their exceptional pitilessness and cruelty!

Finally, the bad times were over, and Ukraine was liberated from the Bolshevik-Jewish yoke. But as it turned out, even when the Communists were gone, the Jews were on hand to continue their dirty business under different slogans. Once more "they took away our economy from us; they trampled on our human rights and burdened us with a new yoke of injustice." In league with their "blood brothers," the Russian "Jew-oligarchs," they took over Ukrainian businesses. Moreover,

> Jewish money bought up all the television channels, which are now, just as in the old [Soviet] times, lying about the guilt of Ukrainians vis-à-vis the Jews. They're lying in an insolent and mean fashion! Contrary to historical evidence they are making Ukrainians into the "greatest anti-Semites." They have robbed us to the bone and are now building a "civil society" in Ukraine. Build one for yourself in Israel! Even if you prostrate yourself before the oppressors, you won't find any pity, compassion, or understanding! There is only one conclusion: nothing can compel the Jews to remove the brand of the "greatest anti-Semites in the world" from the Ukrainians. Even if we gave the Israelites all the riches of Ukraine, they would still leave us with this brand. Now if they could destroy every last Ukrainian, then there would certainly be no one left to be called an anti-Semite!

At this point Demydas' launches a concerted attack on the Kuchma administration and its Jewish manipulators which, in view of the apparent failure of the Orange Revolution and the appointment of Kuchma's tool Yanukovych to prime minister by President Yushchenko in August 2006, may gain renewed relevance in these parts of the country. But what is most striking about this article is the extraordinary expression of resentment, hurt pride, and reversal of images, whereby the Jews are remembered as Ukraine's annihilators and Ukrainians are depicted as the Jews' innocent victims. That this is not merely a view of the past but rather a distorted presentation of the present—informed by and in turn influencing a fantastic, indeed hallucinatory yet intense and powerful image of history—is a clear indication of the inevitable return of the repressed as compulsive obsession. The author's conclusion is simple:

> We have absolutely no doubt that it was Jewish oligarchs who perpetrated a spiritual and economic pogrom in Ukraine on orders from the Moscow special services that they served and are still serving. . . . Buttered bread is tastier, but is it worth the price of serving the Jewish oligarchs who have made Ukraine into a graveyard? Will the ordinary Ukrainian agree to put on the Jewish yoke and to take orders from Moscow's lackeys? Let us be friends with Jews on the ground of brotherly principles. The basis of fraternity must be truth and sincerity.

This extraordinary tirade is especially telling in view of the almost total absence of any Jewish landmarks in contemporary Ternopil'. The only significant indication of the formerly massive Jewish presence in the town is the cemetery, which is located on a hill overlooking the town across the Seret River.[132] This fenced cemetery on Mykulnets'ka Street is only marked by a sign directing those who happen by to the administrative offices of the Ternopil' Oblast' veterans' medical services further down an unmarked side road branching off the main road to the city. The cemetery contains several hundred tombstones dating back to 1903, about three-quarters of which are standing in their original locations. It is not known where the stones removed from the cemetery are located. It also appears that the

---

[132] The following is based on my own visit to the site in June 2004 as well as on "Jewish Cemeteries, Synagogues, and Mass Graves in Ukraine," 24, 50, 94, 119; and on *International Association of Jewish Genealogical Societies— Cemetery Project*, US Commission Reports UA19010101 and UA19010102, http://www.jewishgen.org/cemetery/e-europe/ukra-t.html (accessed December 3, 2006).

FIGURE 48. The Jewish cemetery in Ternopil', 2004.

cemetery contains no mass graves. The ground belongs to the Ternopil' municipality, but the fence that now protects the cemetery was put up only in 1991–94 by the initiative of Ukrainian and foreign Jewish groups, who also see to it that the ground is occasionally, but obviously not regularly, cleared of weeds. An older, sixteenth-century cemetery is known to have existed in town but none of its stones have survived.

Ternopil' was established in 1540 as a private town and during the following century suffered from Cossack, Tatar, and Ottoman attacks.[133] Between the late seventeenth century and

[133] The following is based primarily on *Pinkas Hakehillot*, 234–51, in English, http://www.jewishgen.org/Yizkor/pinkas_poland/pol2_00234.html (accessed December 3, 2006). See also P. Korngruen, ed., *Tarnopol* (Jerusalem: Encyclopedia of the Jewish Diaspora, 1955, in Hebrew). For a memoir see "Additional Readings".

1843 it remained in the possession of the noble Polish Potocki family. Jews are known to have resided in Ternopil' since 1550 and by 1880 they comprised half the total population of the city of almost 26,000. The Jewish population stagnated in the next six decades so that on the eve of World War II there were less than 14,000 Jews in a city with a total population of about 36,000.

Ternopil' was considered exceptional in the early twentieth century for the high degree of tolerance among its Polish, Ukrainian, and Jewish residents. But in the wake of World War I it experienced a pogrom by Ukrainian peasants in 1919. The economic condition of the Jewish population deteriorated in the interwar period, thanks in no small part to the anti-Semitic policies of the Polish government. As elsewhere in the territories taken over by the Soviets in 1939–41, Communist rule was accompanied by the elimination of most Jewish educational and political institutions, expropriation of property, and deportations. While Jewish refugees arrived from German-occupied Poland, the Soviet authorities transferred "hostile" or "unproductive" town dwellers to the surrounding villages. It is estimated that just before the German invasion there were some 17,000 Jews in the city. Only a few hundred of them managed to escape with the retreating Red Army.

Within a couple of days following the German conquest of the city on July 2, 1941, a weeklong pogrom erupted in Ternopil', led by German and Ukrainian police. About a hundred Jews were murdered in a synagogue, which was then set on fire. The discovery of murdered prisoners, shot by the NKVD before fleeing the Wehrmacht, was used as an excuse to massacre the Jews, although among the prisoners executed by the Soviets there were also a number of Jews. The jail became a site of massive torture, humiliation, and butchery. It is reported that while at this point the Germans shot only men, Ukrainian pogromists also killed women and children, using crowbars, axes, and knives. Simultaneously massacres took place also in the surrounding villages; the violence was so intense that eventually the German authorities decided to bring it under control. Altogether during this first week of German occupation some 5,000 Jews, mostly men, were murdered in Ternopil'.

Shortly thereafter the German authorities murdered much of the town's Jewish "intelligentsia" and appointed a Jewish council. A ghetto was established in September and was surrounded by a fence in late 1941. People died there in large numbers due to hunger, cold, and epidemics, while others were employed in forced-labor camps in the area. Some of the workers were forced to use the tombstones of the old Jewish cemetery to pave the road they were building. In March 1942, the first *Aktion* took place, in which about 600–700 Jews, mostly old people and children were shot in a nearby forest by German and Ukrainian policemen. After numerous small-scale executions, a second *Aktion* occurred in August, this time culminating in the deportation of 3,000–4,000 mostly elderly and sick Jews to the Bełżec extermination camp. Another 700 Jews were sent to Bełżec in September. Two more such roundups in November cost the lives of about 2,500 Jews.

In early 1943 there were still about 8,000 Jews in Ternopil', some of whom were employed in a newly built forced-labor camp in the city. But in April a further 1,000 Jews were murdered in a mass shooting, and in June a final *Aktion* followed, after which Ternopil' was declared *Judenrein* but for the Jews employed in the "Julag" (*Judenlager*) labor camp. This camp was in turn liquidated in July, and most of its 2,000–2,500 inmates were killed. The few who managed to escape to the forests were often pursued and murdered by local Ukrainian peasants or denounced to the Germans. On the other hand, there are several known cases in which Ukrainians and Poles sheltered Jews. But only a few hundred Jews survived the war, mostly in exile in the Soviet Union. A memorial put up with permission of the Soviet authorities was destroyed in the 1950s, presumably by orders of the authorities, since simultaneously the two Jewish graveyards in town were also completely destroyed and the sites were used to erect buildings and garages. At the time there was a population of some 500 Jews in the city, mostly from elsewhere, but almost none have remained.

Hardly a trace of past Jewish presence or a reminder of its bloody end can be found in Ternopil'. The extraordinary fortress synagogue built in the seventeenth century has vanished, and the municipality provides no indication as to where it was located, although the ruin was still standing at the end of the war. The local history museum contained a vehemently nationalist and anti-Soviet historical exhibition in March 2003, but not a single mention of former Jewish life—or death—in Ternopil'. The previous year the museum had apparently exhibited a glass cabinet containing a few Jewish items, but when we asked about this display, a museum attendant commented that it had merely been a temporary exhibit.

Possibly the only mention of the annihilation of Jewish life in Ternopil' is a plaque inscribed in Yiddish and Ukrainian located by the main door of the medical faculty building. The reference in the text to "fascists" dates it back to Soviet times. But while the Yiddish speaks of "thousands of Tarnopol Jews" shot there in early July 1941, the Ukrainian version mentions only "hundreds." There is, however, no paucity of memorials and commemorative plaques in Ternopil', all dedicated to the persecution of Ukrainians by the Soviets and to glorifying local nationalist fighters. Thus the gymnasium in central Ternopil' carries a plaque commemorating one of its students, UPA Major "Yahoda" "Chernyk" (these two names were his wartime aliases) Mar'ian Lukasevych, born in 1922 and a student at the school in 1930–37, who was killed in September 1945, most probably by the Soviets.

As we saw in Monastyrys'ka, Ternopil' too has a commemorative portrait mural of famous twentieth-century Ukrainians. Surprisingly, among the six we also find Agnon, depicted wearing a black skullcap and described as a Hebrew writer. With this fleeting and not unambiguous nod to Jewish life in Ukraine the sun sets behind the town castle, and hundreds of birds circle over our heads in the darkening sky. We retire to the vast empty Soviet hotel, located not far from the Jewish cemetery, and watch from our windows as the last rays of light set fire to the numerous church steeples that dot the city across the river.

Berezhany / Brzeżany/ Brizan

FIGURE 49. The Great Synagogue of Berezhany, 2004.

NOT FAR from Ternopil', heading southwest, lies the town of Berezhany. In 2002 an Israeli historian published a book, part memoir and part history, that described his survival as a young boy in that town during the German occupation.[134] The author, Shimon Redlich, was saved by Ukrainians and Poles, and in his book expresses thanks and admiration for his rescuers. He also points out that many of those who helped did so for reasons of

---

[134] Shimon Redlich, *Together and Apart in Brzeżany: Poles, Jews, and Ukrainians, 1919–1945* (Bloomington: Indiana University Press, 2002).

greed, while others had more altruistic motivations. While he makes a heroic effort to be fair and balanced, Redlich cannot avoid but point out the collaboration of many Ukrainians in the murder of the Jewish population of his hometown: of approximately 10,000 Jews who lived there when the Germans marched in, less than 100 survived.[135]

Unlike the controversy in Poland over Jan Tomasz Gross's book *Neighbors*, which reconstructed the murder of the Jewish population of the eastern Polish town of Jedwabne by its Polish inhabitants, the publication of Redlich's book in Ukrainian did not cause much of a storm.[136] This probably indicates that in Ukraine public discourse has not even reached the point of acknowledging the immense tragedy of the Holocaust, let alone openly discussing Ukrainian complicity in the mass murder of the Jews. Rather, these events are often distorted in ways meant to gain other political and ideological ends. This was nicely illustrated by an article published in the Ternopil' newspaper *Vil'ne zhyttia* (Free Life), which expressed the historical perspective of Ukrainian nationalist ideology.[137]

The author of the essay, Dariya Shatna, claims that Redlich had not used objective archival documentation on events in Berezhany and instead relied on biased accounts and testimonies. The result is, she writes, that Redlich himself expresses bigoted opinions about Ukrainians. She is especially troubled because the book's "racist characterization of Ukrainians and its hyperbolic falsifications regarding the 'Jewish pogrom in Berezhany,' [and] the actions of the 'Ukrainian bandits,'"

---

[135] Ibid., 113.

[136] Gross, *Neighbors*; Polonsky and Michlic, *Neighbors Respond*.

[137] Dariya Shatna, "V im'ya istorychnoï spravedlyvosti bud'mo ob'yektyvnymy i pravdyvymy" [Let's Be Objective and Truthful in the Name of Historical Justice], *Vil'ne zhyttia*, no. 37, April 15, 2004.

threaten to "create a universally negative image of Ukraine." This is all the more disturbing to Shatna because the book "has appeared in English, Polish, and Ukrainian," and is described on its cover as "going far beyond the local context and regional history."[138] A "refutation of this falsification" is necessary, she writes, since such unjust allegations against Ukrainians subject them to "moral discrimination," by which she implies that Ukrainians are being blamed for the crimes of the Germans and for this reason are mistreated by the rest of the world.[139]

But Shatna is not only worried by the false image of Ukraine; she also wants to expose the real face of the Jews. Thus she asserts that the Jews have always collaborated with whichever regime or ethnic group was in power. Consequently, the Jews also dominated the NKVD, and therefore they collaborated with the Soviets in the genocide of the Ukrainians. For this reason Jews are hardly in a position to blame the Ukrainians for

---

[138] Redlich's book was published in Polish as *Razem i osobno: Polacy, Żydzi, Ukraińcy w Brzeżanach 1919–1945* (Sejny: Pogranicze, 2002); in Ukrainian as *Razom i narizno v Berezhanakh: Poliaky, yevreï ta ukraïntsi, 1919–1945* (Kyiv: Dukh i litera, 2002); and in Hebrew by Ben Gurion University Press in Beer-Sheva in 2005.

[139] This is somewhat reminiscent of complaints lodged over the years by Polish commentators arguing that because the Germans built extermination camps in Poland there has been a tendency to blame Poles for the Holocaust. To be sure, the choice of Poland as a killing site by the Germans had little to do with the Poles. Conversely, perfectly legitimate references to Polish martyrdom and suffering under the Germans—and in German camps—have been employed over the years to obfuscate Polish collaboration in and expressions of support for the "removal" of Jews from Poland. See, e.g., Joshua D. Zimmerman, ed., *Contested Memories: Poles and Jews during the Holocaust and its Aftermath* (New Brunswick, N.J.: Rutgers University Press, 2003); Antony Polonsky, ed., *My Brother's Keeper? Recent Polish Debates on the Holocaust* (London: Routledge, 1990).

collaborating with the Nazis in the Holocaust.[140] Concluding her article with an account of the crimes perpetrated by the Bolsheviks (read the Jews) against the Ukrainians, Shatna rhetorically calls for a second Nuremberg Tribunal, this time for the genocide of the Ukrainians, in which, it is implied, the Jews will play the role of the indicted.[141]

[140] In a speech made on October 3, 2003, the German CDU representative Martin Hohmann argued that the Jews were in no position to blame the Germans collectively for the Holocaust since the Jews could also be described as a *Tätervolk* (nation of perpetrators), thanks to their high representation among the Bolsheviks who committed mass murders akin to those of the Nazis. There are obvious similarities between Hohmann's and Shatna's line of argumentation, which is typical of right-wing and nationalist militant apologetics. For the text of the speech, see "Die Rede zum Nationalfeiertag, am 3. Oktober 2003," http://www.hagalil.com/archiv/2003/11/hohmann-3.htm (accessed August 17, 2006). For a nuanced analysis of Jewish involvement with communism and the Soviet Union, see Yuri Slezkine, *The Jewish Century* (Princeton: Princeton University Press, 2004).

[141] One result of this article has been that my collaborator in Buchach, suspecting that I too would defame the good name of the Ukrainian people, has become much more reluctant to help me and has asked explicitly that I do not mention his name in any future publications. I respect his request, also because he seems to fear retaliation from other residents; but I would like nevertheless to thank him for providing me with a great deal of invaluable material. Apart from Redlich, see *Pinkas Hakehillot*, 107–14 for the history of the town and the events of the Holocaust. See also Menachem Katz, ed., *Brzeżany, Narajow, and their Surroundings: A History of Destroyed Communities* (Haifa: Association of Former Residents of Brzeżany, Narajow, and their Surroundings in Israel and the United States, 1978, in Hebrew and Yiddish with an English summary) partial translation into English, http://www.jewishgen.org/Yizkor/berezhany/berezhany.html (accessed December 3, 2006), scanned copy, http://yizkor.nypl.org/index.php?id=2312 (accessed December 3, 2006). See also "*wikipedia* S.V. "Brzezany," http://en.wikipedia.org/wiki/Brzezany (accessed December 3, 2006); "*Słownik Geograficzny* Entry: Brzeżany, "*Polish Roots*" http://www.polishroots.org/slownik/brzezany.htm (accessed December 3, 2006).

This extreme perspective is not shared by all, or even most Ukrainians, certainly not if we take into account the country as a whole rather than only its western and most nationalist provinces. Quite apart from those who undertook the translation and publication of Redlich's book, there were others who welcomed it precisely because it served as proof, to their minds, of the prevalence of "good Ukrainians" and therefore helped to further disseminate what can be called the "Sheptyts'kyi cult." Indeed, while not sharing this cult, Redlich himself has made a significant contribution to the recognition of Metropolitan Andrei Sheptyts'kyi's efforts to save Jews during the Holocaust and has led a long and as yet unsuccessful campaign for his recognition as a "righteous gentile" by Yad Vashem in Jerusalem.[142] Arguably this quest for "good" Ukrainians might

---

[142] Metropolitan Andrei Sheptyts'kyi of L'viv was a Ukrainian national leader who initially welcomed the invasion of the Germans to Soviet-occupied Western Ukraine but later denounced the Holocaust and saved as many as 150 Jews or more. See Shimon Redlich, "Metropolitan Andrei Sheptyts'kyi, Ukrainians and Jews During and After the Holocaust," *Holocaust and Genocide Studies* 5, no. 1 (1990): 39–51; Redlich, "Sheptyts'kyi and the Jews during World War II," in *Morality and Reality: The Life and Times of Andrei Sheptyts'kyi,* ed. Paul Robert Magocsi (Edmonton: Canadian Institute of Ukrainian Studies, University of Alberta, 1989), 145–62. On recent activities intended to commemorate Sheptyts'kyi as a heroic "good Ukrainian," see Yossi Melman and Asaf Carmel, "The Ukrainian Schindler," *Haaretz Magazine,* September 9, 2005, 58–62, in English, http://www.haaretz.com/hasen/pages/ShArt.jhtml?itemNo=632512&contrassID=19 (accessed December 3, 2006). On November 7, 2005 an event dedicated to Sheptyts'kyi was organized in L'viv by the TKUMA Central Ukrainian Holocaust Foundation (Dnepropetrovsk), the L'viv Holocaust International Center, and the American Jewish Joint Distribution Committee. See "Metropolitan Andrei Sheptytsky International Scientific Conference," *Tkuma All-Ukrainian Center for Holocaust Studies,* http://tkuma.dp.ua/en/index.php?option=com_content&task=view&id=11&Itemid=17 (accessed December 3, 2006). See also Andrew Thomas Kanie, "Andrii Sheptyts'kyi: His Brother's Keeper," *Church & Life,*

be a more representative trend. Moreover, a few Ukrainian historians have given qualified praise to Redlich's book, even as they criticize him for being one-sided, and have more generally offered a more nuanced view of Soviet rule and Jewish "collaboration."[143] Nevertheless, the fact remains that especially in Western Ukraine it is still possible to argue not merely for an equivalence of suffering but to shift the burden of guilt from Ukrainian collaboration in the Holocaust to Jewish participation and indeed leadership in the mass murder of Ukrainians by the Bolshevik authorities.

---

no. 36 (August 31–September 6, 1998): 4, http://catholicukes.org.au/tiki/tiki-download_file.php?fileId3 (accessed December 3, 2006); Himka, "Ukrainian Collaboration." The metropolitan's brother, Klemens Sheptyts'kyi, was recognized by Yad Vashem as a "righteous gentile" for organizing this rescue of the Jews. See Anne Sebba, "He did all that was possible—he saved 150 Jews," *Times Higher Education Supplement,* January 27, 2006, http://www.annesebba.com/journalist/prof_redlich.htm (accessed December 3, 2006).

[143] See, e.g., "Soviet Totalitarianism in Ukraine: History and Legacy," Conference organized by the book review magazine *Krytyka,* Kyiv, September 2–6, 2005; and Andriy Portnov, "Pochuty inshoho" [To Hear the Other] *Krytyka* 7–8 (July–August): 5, http://krytyka.kiev.ua/articles/s2_7-8_2003.html (accessed December 3, 2006). While Portnov praises Redlich for recognizing that "every national group focused on its own suffering and persecution and remained almost deaf to the suffering of other groups" he also remarks that Redlich himself was "not always free of prejudices." Further on current Ukrainian politics of history, see Jilge, "Politics," a Ukrainian version of which has appeared in *Krytyka* 5, no. 103 (May 2006): 19–22; Andriy Portnov, "Presenting the Past: Comments on History Textbooks in Belarus, Russia and Ukraine," in *Ukraine's Re-Integration into Europe: A Historical, Historiographical and Politically Urgent Issue,* ed. Giovanna Brogi Bercoff and Giulia Lami (Alessandria: Edizioni dell'Orso, 2005), 325–35; Georgiy Kasianov, "The Burden of the Past: The Ukrainian-Polish Conflict of 1943–44 in Contemporary Public, Academic and Political Debates in Ukraine and Poland," http://www.iccr-international.org/euro/docs/paper-kasianov.pdf (accessed December 3, 2006).

Figure 50. Berezhany town map, 2004.

The enterprising mayor of Berezhany has now renovated the center of the town, after years of neglect under Soviet rule. The Ukrainian Holy Trinity Church, the municipal hall, and the square that separates them have been tastefully repaired, repainted, and paved. On a cold March afternoon in 2003, under a bright blue sky, the town evinced an air of hope and progress. The mayor had also obligingly put up a town map in the central square, where all the main sites were clearly marked. But there was no indication of any former Jewish sites. Berezhany is not a large town, and we believed that someone would be able to point us to the synagogue, which we knew from Redlich's book was not destroyed. Most people on the street seemed to have no idea, until we found a young lad, who not only led us down the short path to what has remained of the synagogue, but also claimed to know where Redlich had lived and to recall his visit to his hometown some years back.

Redlich provides a photograph of the Great Synagogue as it looked in 1991. While it was an empty shell, it still retained the basic shape and structure that can be glimpsed from prewar photographs. Twelve years later very little of this shell was left. Barely two walls were standing, and they too seemed to be very close to collapse. The ground was littered with garbage. The synagogue, after all, is not in some isolated spot out of town, but a few minutes' walk from the main square (the German-imposed ghetto was just behind the square). Ironically, a standard plaque has been attached to one of the two remaining walls, noting that this is a protected architectural monument, and that anyone causing it damage could be prosecuted. Otherwise one can find no mention of the past existence of Jews in Berezhany, let alone a memorial commemorating their murder. In the 1930s, Jews comprised about a third of the total population. Today, it may be difficult for the population to grasp why such a large and impressive synagogue once stood so close to the center of town, but this riddle will soon be solved by the forces of nature and human neglect.

Berezhany does boast both a Soviet memorial, built at the edge of the Christian cemetery, and a monument to the men of the UPA that faces the Soviet edifice in an understandably hostile attitude, considering that for much of its existence the latter dedicated itself to fighting the former. The *okopisko*, or Jewish cemetery, in which thousands of the Jewish residents were murdered, carries no such memorial. Conversely, Berezhany recently decided to celebrate its six-hundred-and-thirtieth anniversary by erecting a monument with a bust of OUN-B leader Stepan

Bandera.[144] Thus once more—and despite Redlich's efforts at reconciliation through history and truth—rather than providing a space to the memory and tragedy of the Jewish community of the town, Berezhany will soon celebrate the man whose organization called for the "removal" of the Jews and whose loyal troops helped bring it about.

[144] See *Ternopil's'ka hazeta*, July 5, 2005, http://www.te-ga.com/index. php?story=9271 (accessed December 3, 2006).

165

FIGURE 51. Panel of Ukrainian NKVD victims in Zolochiv citadel museum, 2004.

Zolochiv / Złoczów / Zlotshev

In 1999 a public controversy in Germany ended up with the closing of a traveling exhibition that had been visited by about 800,000 Germans and Austrians over the preceding four years. The exhibition presented over a thousand photographs, mostly taken by German soldiers, of atrocities committed by the Wehrmacht and related organizations and allies against prisoners of war, partisans, and Jews. This was a shocking revelation to many Germans. To be sure, ever since the 1960s scholars had documented the involvement of regular German military units and the higher echelons of the armed forces in Nazi genocidal policies. But there was a vast difference between heavy tomes gathering dust on library shelves and stark photographs publicly exhibited in one's own town.[145]

Some of the photographs concerned atrocities committed in Eastern Galician towns that were overrun by the Wehrmacht in July 1941, such as L'viv, Ternopil', and Zolochiv. The German debate showed little interest in or knowledge of the nature and history of the Jewish communities of these towns that were

---

[145] See Hamburg Institute for Social Research, ed., *The German Army and Genocide: Crimes Against War Prisoners, Jews, and Other Civilians, 1939–1944* (New York: New Press, 1999); Omer Bartov, "The Wehrmacht Exhibition Controversy: The Politics of Evidence," in *Crimes of War: Guilt and Denial in the Twentieth Century*, ed. Omer Bartov, Atina Grossmann, and Mary Nolan (New York: New Press, 2002), 41–60; Bartov, *Germany's War and the Holocaust: Disputed Histories* (Ithaca: Cornell University Press, 2003), pt. 1.

about to be wiped out over the following few years. Characteristically for present-day Germany, this was a debate over German crimes, not about the victims of these crimes. But in the fall of 1999 it was revealed that the context of these atrocities made the identities of both perpetrators and victims less clear than the photographs had seemed to indicate. Photographs, of course, do not speak for themselves; in order to know who is featured in them and what the sequence of events that led to and followed the single instant imprinted on the film is, we must be able to reconstruct the context.

Thanks especially to the Polish-German scholar Bogdan Musial, it was discovered that photographs from several Eastern Galician towns depicted not Jewish victims of the German army, SS, and Gestapo, but rather mostly Ukrainian victims of the NKVD, who were butchered just before the Red Army retreated from the region in early July 1941.[146] Or at least, this was the original claim, which finally led to a closing of the exhibition and an inquiry into the veracity of its claims. Closer inspection over the following year indicated that in fact the photographs encompassed the entire tragic story of late June and early July 1941. In several cases they did indeed show the corpses of political prisoners (who also included Poles and Jews), murdered by the Soviets and exhumed by Jewish residents of these towns,

[146] Bogdan Musial, "Bilder einer Ausstellung. Kritische Anmerkungen zur Wanderausstellung 'Vernichtungskrieg. Verbrechen der Wehrmacht 1941 bis 1944,'" in *Vierteljahrshefte für Zeitgeschichte* 47 (1999): 563–91. See also Krisztián Ungváry, "Echte Bilder—problematische Aussagen. Eine quantitative und qualitative Analyse des Bildmaterials der Ausstellung 'Vernichtungskrieg. Verbrechen der Wehrmacht 1941 bis 1944,'" and Dieter Schmidt-Neuhaus, "Die Tarnopol-Stellwand der Wanderausstellung 'Vernichtungskrieg. Verbrechen der Wehrmacht 1941 bis 1944.' Eine Falluntersuchung zur Verwendung von Bildquellen," both in *Geschichte in Wissenschaft und Unterricht* 10 (1999): 584–95 and 596–603, respectively.

whom local Ukrainian nationalists and newly arrived German units accused of being responsible for these killings. The photos also showed the bodies of Jews who had been beaten to death or shot immediately after exhuming these bodies by the Germans or their Ukrainian collaborators as "punishment" for their alleged crimes. Hence the photos also carried evidence of the wave of pogroms, instigated by local nationalists as well as the *Einsatzgruppen* (mobile murder squads of the SS and SD) in the early days of the German occupation, which cost the lives of thousands of primarily Jewish men.[147]

This is indeed what occurred in Zolochiv, which is located some 20 miles north of Berezhany.[148] Established as a town in

---

[147] Omer Bartov, Cornelia Brink, Gerhard Hirschfeld, Friedrich P. Kahlenberg, Manfred Messerschmidt, Reinhard Rürup, Christian Streit, Hans-Ulrich Thamer, *Bericht der Kommission zur Überprüfung der Ausstellung "Vernichtungskrieg. Verbrechen der Wehrmacht 1941 bis 1944"* (November 2000), http://www.his-online.de/download/Kommissionsbericht.pdf (accessed December 3, 2006).

[148] For background on these events, see Bernd Boll, "Złoczów, July 1941: The Wehrmacht and the Beginning of the Holocaust in Galicia: From a Criticism of Photographs to a Revision of the Past," in Bartov et al., *Crimes of War*, 61–99, http://www.weiterdenken.de/download/Zloczow(ZfG).pdf (accessed December 3, 2006); Bechtel, "De Jedwabne à Zolotchiv"; Musial, *"Konterrevolutionäre Elemente,"* 179–85; Baruch Karu and El. Boneh, eds., *The Book of the Zloczow Community* (Tel Aviv: Association of Former Zloczow Residents, 1967, in Hebrew), esp. 153–55 (Dr. Altman), 184–191 (Shlomo Meir), and English version with separate title in the back of the same volume: I. M. Lask and El. Boneh, eds., *The City of Zloczow* (Zoloczower Relief Verband of America, 1967), esp. 29–43; Shlomo Wolkowicz, *The Mouth of Hell* (Haverford, Pa.: Infinity, 2002), 20–34; Samuel Lipa Tennenbaum, *Złoczów Memoir, 1939–1944: A Chronicle of Survival* (New York: Shengold Publishers, 1986), 167–77; Ephraim F. Sten, *1111 Days in My Life Plus Four*, trans. Moshe Dor (Takoma Park, Md.: Dryad Press, 2006), 3–20. Remarkably, throughout the debate over the Wehrmacht Exhibition no one bothered to look up the detailed accounts by survivors of these events in the memorial books of the relevant towns.

1523, Zolochiv is known to have had a Jewish presence as of the mid-sixteenth century, which on the eve of World War I swelled to almost half of the total population of just over 12,000 inhabitants. With the outbreak of World War II large numbers of Jewish refugees from western Poland fled to the city, but many of them were deported by the Soviet occupiers to the interior of the USSR, while numerous young men were conscripted into the Red Army. It is estimated that at the time there were some 10,000 Jews in the city along with another 10,000 Poles and Ukrainians. The Germans marched into Zolochiv on July 1, 1941. Upon discovering the mass graves of some 600 political prisoners murdered by the NKVD, the SS as well as regular German army soldiers along with the Ukrainians and Poles in the town unleashed a pogrom that lasted three days. Estimates of the number of Jews murdered in the city's citadel—where the bodies of the political prisoners were found—and in the streets of the city range between 1,000 and 4,000.

Together with other victims of massacres in nearby villages it is estimated that the total number of Jewish victims of these first days of the German occupation reached as high as 5,000. Mass killing resumed in late August 1942, when about 2,700

For an important exception, see Marco Carynnyk's book, tentatively titled *Furious Angles: Ukrainians, Jews, and Poles in the Summer of 1941* (New Haven: Yale University Press, forthcoming), and his article, "Zolochiv movchyt'" [Zolochiv is Silent] in *Krytyka* 10 (2005), http://krytyka.kiev.ua/articles/s.5_10_2005.html (accessed December 3, 2006). For a succinct history, see *Pinkas Hakehillot*, 217–24, English translation, http://www.jewishgen.org/Yizkor/pinkas_poland/pol2_00217.html (accessed December 3, 2006). For a Polish-centric account that avoids this bloody history, see "Dawne Kresy" (obecna Ukraina): Złoczów, http://www.amigo.wroc.pl/ukraina/zloczow.htm (accessed December 3, 2006). The town's official Ukrainian website makes no mention of these events: see "Zolochiv page," http://zl.lv.ukrtel.net/index1.html (accessed December 3, 2006).

FIGURE 52. Inner court and palace in Zolochiv citadel, 2004.

Jews were deported to the Bełżec extermination camp. A second *Aktion* cost the lives of a further 2,500 Jews taken to Bełżec in early November. The ghetto established in December contained between 7,500 and 9,000 people, including many brought there from nearby communities. It was liquidated in April 1943, at which point about 6,000 people were taken to a nearby village and murdered in mass shootings. Most of the Jews who managed to hide were discovered and murdered over the next few months, including several small resistance groups that tried to find shelter in the forests. The town was liberated in July 1944, but only a handful of survivors were still living there.

Contemporary Zolochiv has a very partial memory of these events. Visiting the town's citadel in March 2003, I found there

171

a modest exhibition dedicated exclusively to the discovery and exhumation of the political prisoners murdered by the NKVD. The citadel was at the time under renovation, but as recent photos indicate, this work has now been completed. One assumes that the bones of the thousands of Jews murdered there are still buried under the elegant courtyard with its garden and fountain. As for the stark exhibit located in one of the citadel's other buildings, while it was obviously put up after the fall of the Communist regime, it still has all the hallmarks of Soviet propaganda and style; all that has changed is the emphasis. Visitors are confronted with a few photographs of the exhumed bodies, neatly arranged in rows (this work was done by Jews, a fact that is not mentioned in the exhibit), some photos of the victims, and several lists of names. Most important, several panels carry testimonies given decades later of the events surrounding the discovery of the bodies. Not a single mention is made of the brutal pogrom that followed.

Thus, one of the panels carries a testimony given in 1995:

> When the Germans entered Zolochiv and opened the prison, no one was alive in them. All the prisoners had been murdered in a bestial and cruel manner. All the murdered people were thrown out of a window into a big pit. All of them were exhumed and arranged in rows, so that their parents would recognize them. But it was impossible to recognize any of them. Mama recognized Father by his boots—which were lined—and by his pants.

The text of another panel is taken from the memoirs of an eyewitness published in 1960, but originally printed in a Ukrainian newspaper in German-occupied L'viv in 1941:

> In the Zolochiv prison were found 649 people who had been bestially tortured to death. In a pit outside the prison 432 people were dug up. They had been drenched with gasoline and burned, and for that reason only some of the bodies could be

172

identified. In another pit in the courtyard 217 people were dug up. These were only the victims of the last few days before the Bolsheviks fled from Zolochiv.

Further panels describe the fates of other victims and attempts by their families to preserve their memory for many decades thereafter. Thus Oleksiy Yarosh, a resident of the village of Pomoriany, was arrested on June 24, 1941. According to a 1995 testimony,

> No one saw him alive again. His own wife could not recognize him among the victims. Distraught, she entered the building where the offices appeared to have been located, and among the papers scattered about in the dust she found her husband's documents . . . which indicated his arrest. She guarded these documents like a precious treasure, because they were stained with Oleksiy's blood. She took them with her to Siberia, where she hid them several times in the ground in order to save them.

The final panel introduces the list of names:

> Today we search for the names of those whose death in June 1941 revealed to us the essence of this terrible regime. . . . The organizers of this exhibition put a special caption: "time and place of death." And for all of them the words are the same: Zolochiv prison, 1941.[149]

These are stories of pain, sorrow, suffering, and loss. But as is the case in many other sites of atrocity in the world and over many centuries, the urge to remember and commemorate is tightly bound with the need to suppress and forget. We stand on the soil in which thousands of Zolochiv's Jewish inhabitants are buried. We are summoned to remember. But the memory of the martyrs we are called upon to commemorate must not be

[149] Thanks to Delphine Bechtel and Marco Carynnyk for assistance with the translation of these texts and for much valuable advice and information.

sullied by the memory of those whom so many of the martyrs' grieving family members had helped to murder. The fortress has been transformed into a site of memory, and simultaneously, into a black hole of selective, pitiless amnesia. As an account by S. Altman, one of the few survivors of the Jewish community, reveals, the discovery of the NKVD victims was only the beginning of the horror, not its conclusion:

> Crowds armed with axes, hatchets, shovels, iron bars, hammers, and firearms simultaneously stormed all the Jewish streets and houses, dragging their occupants into the streets. The pogrom began from preselected places ... but the main center of operations was the Citadel. Hordes of Ukrainians and SS-men swooped down upon their defenseless victims with whatever they had in their hands .... Ukrainian neighbors, with whom only the day before there had been friendly or business relations, were now relentless enemies. They lured Jews into their homes only to hand them over to the savage mob. When the wave of terror eventually died down, people were found drowned in latrines and sewage holes, some with chopped-off heads. A number of scoundrels had caught Rabbi Ellenberg, tied him to a motorcycle with a rope and dragged him up the street ... [until] the venerable old man fell from exhaustion and his body was dragged along, mutilated and unrecognizable. In another part of town a number of Jews were forced to exhume the Ukrainian corpses from the grave, wash them, carry them out of the yard and arrange them in rows. Many, women and children among them, could not go through with this terrible ordeal and fainted with the horror and the stench. These were mercilessly beaten and killed on the spot. Meanwhile others were brought and ordered to jump into the now empty graves, where they were machine-gunned by the SS-men. Without bothering whether the victims were alive or dead, they were covered with the new people and the procedure was repeated. The screams of the wounded and those buried alive rose to heaven but none heeded

them. On that day Jewish blood flowed like a river . . . . Many German officers watched the pogrom with calm cynicism, clicking their cameras all the time. A few months later I happened to come across some of these photographs in an illustrated German weekly. One of them depicted a scene at the citadel, with women weeping over a pile of corpses. Among these I definitely recognized Luisa Freimann, the daughter of Shyjo and Dziunka Kitaj. The scene bore the caption "Ukrainian women mourning their husbands, who were murdered by the Jews."[150]

[150] Lask and Boneh, *Zloczow*, 38–42. For similar photos of identification and mourning whose captions may not accurately describe the events taking place and the identities of the protagonists, see, e.g., Musial, *"Konterrevolutionäre Elemente,"* 176–77; Boshyk, *Ukraine during World War II*, photos between pp. 108 and 109.

Brody / Brodie / Brod / Prode

FIGURE 53. Monument to famous sons of Brody next to the gymnasium, 2004.

THE TOWN of Brody, some 20 miles northeast of Zolochiv, is quite close to the old Russian border. Founded in 1584 as a private town, Brody was heavily damaged in wars and fires in the seventeenth and eighteenth centuries, but eventually emerged as an important urban and economic center.[151] The city was

---

[151] For an outline of the city's Jewish history, see *Pinkas Hakehillot*, 121–34. See also Aviv Meltzer, ed., *Eternal Light: Brody in Memoriam. A Memory Volume to Brody and Its Vicinity* (Jerusalem: Association of Former Brody Residents in Israel, 1994, in Hebrew, Yiddish, and English), partial translation, http://www.jewishgen.org/yizkor/brody/brody.html (accessed, December 3,

inhabited by Jews from its very beginning and their numbers rose as it became a locus for Jewish refugees fleeing from the Turkish and Cossack wars. As early as 1799 the Jewish population of the city reached over 14,000 people, or 86 percent of the total number of inhabitants. Already considered one of the wealthiest and economically most successful Jewish communities in the region before the annexation of Galicia by the Habsburg Empire in 1772, by the early decades of the nineteenth century Brody was known as "the Jewish Amsterdam of the East," and became a major gateway for the fur trade between Siberia and the fairs of Leipzig. But the city declined precipitously in the latter part of the century thanks to the construction of a railway line into Russia that passed through another town, and by the early twentieth century it had become one of the poorest towns in northeastern Galicia. By 1910 the Jewish population of Brody had declined to 12,000 out of a total of 18,000 inhabitants.

Brody was occupied for a while by the Russians in World War I and suffered severe damage in the fighting. Jews were harassed and deported by the Russian army, and were subsequently targeted for attacks also during the short-lived Ukrainian republic of 1919, as well as being subjected to discriminatory policies by

---

2006); Nathan Michael Gelber, *History of the Jews of Brody 1584–1943* (Jerusalem: Rav Kuk Institute, 1955, in Hebrew); Yakov Khonigsman, *Yevreyi goroda Brody: 1584–1944* [Jews of the City of Brody] (L'viv: L'vovskoe obshchestvo yevreiskoi kul'tury im. Sholom-Aleikhem, 2001). For a report on a recent visit to Brody see Ruhama Elbag, "Brody between the Lines," *Haaretz*, September 7, 2004 (in Hebrew). See further in Roman Zakharii, "Galician Jerusalem: Brody as Jewish Intellectual and Cultural Hub of Eastern Galicia," http://www.personal.ceu.hu/students/97/Roman_Zakharii/brody.doc (accessed December 3, 2006); "Brody," http://www.shtetlinks.jewishgen.org/Brody/Brody.htm (accessed December 3, 2006); "Brody, Ukraine: Maps," http://www.lisashea.com/genealogy/eva/maps.html (accessed December 3, 2006).

the conquering Poles.[152] By the time Polish rule was established in 1920 the population of the city had declined to 10,000 inhabitants, of whom 7,000 were Jews. Under the Soviet occupation of 1939–41 businesses were nationalized, political parties were broken up, and many Jewish economic and political leaders were deported to the interior of the Soviet Union.

Brody was occupied by the Germans in early July 1941. After a couple of weeks, about 250 members of the Jewish intelligentsia were arrested, tortured, and shot next to burial pits in the Jewish cemetery. During winter 1941 the Germans frequently raided the part of town where the Jews were increasingly concentrated and took some 1,500 people to forced labor in surrounding camps, where most perished. Conditions in the town were abysmal, and hunger and epidemics took a high toll. The first mass deportation occurred in mid-September 1942, with up to 2,500 taken to Bełżec and several hundred shot in the streets. In November another 2,000–3,000 were deported to Bełżec. The houses vacated by the victims were taken up by Jews brought to Brody from the surrounding villages and towns. A ghetto was established in December 1942 and liquidated in late May 1943. About 3,500 Jews were deported to Majdanek or possibly to Sobibór, several hundred were shot on the spot, and the ghetto was burned down. Many Jews appear to have been murdered in the forest near the "new" Jewish cemetery. Only about 250 of the original Jewish population survived, of whom less than a hundred had been sheltered by local Ukrainians and Poles, as well as by a few Germans, some of whom paid dearly for their altruism.

Nowadays Brody contains very few reminders of this past. A couple of streets down from the main city square the empty

---

[152] Ansky, *Enemy*, 66–71; Alexander Victor Prusin, *Nationalizing a Borderland: War, Ethnicity, and Anti-Jewish Violence in East Galicia, 1914–1920* (Tuscaloosa: University of Alabama Press, 2005), 55–62, 105. See further in "Additional Readings."

FIGURE 54. The Old Fortress Synagogue, Brody, 2004.

shell of the Old Fortress Synagogue can still be found. In mid-July 1944 the Red Army encircled and destroyed eight German divisions in the vicinity of Brody, including the SS–Galicia Division which was made up of Ukrainian recruits.[153] The Germans tried to blow up the synagogue but thanks to its robust construction it remained standing. The walls of this imposing structure, built in 1742 and supported by scaffolding from within, are covered with graffiti; it is hard to believe that it will remain standing for long. No sign indicates its history or what

---

[153] Subtelny, *Ukraine*, 477. Of the 10,000 men serving at the time in the Galician Division some 3,000 were killed, wounded, or captured. About 5,000 managed to break out of the encirclement and an estimated 2,000 eluded captivity and later joined the UPA.

FIGURE 55. Brody's Golden Street, 2004.

it symbolizes for a city that for much of its existence had a majority Jewish population. Again, this is not due to any dearth of a culture of memory. Indeed, the city square boasts two memorials. One features a bronze bust of the UPA ideologue Petro Poltava, set on a granite base and, during my visit in June 2004, decorated with fresh wreaths of flowers. Another starker, cross-shaped monument is dedicated to Ukrainian victims of Soviet persecution and contains samples of soil from numerous gulags as an evocation of the town's martyred sons, buried in the far reaches of the former Soviet Union.[154]

[154] Attempts to commemorate that controversial past began right after the end of Communist rule in Ukraine. See O. Telenchi, "One Is Building,

From these monuments one heads down what used to be called ulica Złota, or Golden Street—now renamed in Ukrainian vulytsia Zolota—once an elegant boulevard where the wealthier Jewish merchants lived. The Jewish writer Sholem Aleichem was so impressed with this street, dotted with cafés and restaurants, when he passed through Brody on his way to the United States in 1905, that he called the town a "true garden of Eden." Nowadays one can still detect some elegant porches, but decades of Soviet rule and the current poverty of the region have ensured that there is hardly any echo of the lively atmosphere described by pre–World War I travelers, featured for instance in Agnon's novel *The Bridal Canopy*.[155] Nor will one find any mention of Jews, apart from the humble, single-story synagogue or *shtibel* that still stands nearby, bearing no indication of its former identity.

Another Is Destroying," *Holos Ukraïny*, May 31, 1991, 4–5, reporting that "at the village of Yaseniv in the Brody district a memorial was unveiled to the victims of World War II, including the soldiers who perished in the 'Brody cauldron.' The construction of the memorial was initiated by the L'viv Students Association. The stele carries the emblem of the SS-Galicia division." In its June 19, 1991 edition, however, the same paper reported (p. 5) that "Before dawn on June 18 a powerful explosion was heard in the village of Yaseniv," in which "the recently unveiled memorial was blown up . . . . According to the chief of Brody's district militia department . . . the memorial was completely destroyed." Nevertheless, an elaborate memorial now exists in the vicinity of Yaseniv, near Brody, dedicated to the SS-Galicia Division and to its "3,000 officers, NCOs, and soldiers," who, "after breaking out of the encirclement near Brody . . . continued fighting against the [Soviet] occupiers within the [ranks of] the UPA." See http://www.mycastles.com.ua/index.php?id=halychyna (accessed December 3, 2006). Meanwhile, in 2005 President Viktor Yushchenko unveiled a memorial to the Ukrainian Galician Army (UHA) of 1918–19. See Zenon Zawada, "Presidents of Ukraine and Poland Unveil memorials at Lviv Cemetery," *Ukranian Weekly*, July 3, 2005, http://www.ukrweekly.com/Archive/2005/270501.shtml (accessed December 3, 2006).

[155] For full citation see "Additional Readings."

FIGURE 56. Joseph Roth's gymnasium in Brody, 2004.

At the bottom of Golden Street we reach the handsome Brody Gymnasium building, built in 1881 and formerly named after the Habsburg Archduke Rudolf. Here a feeble attempt has been made to integrate memories, though it does not go much farther than what we have seen in Drohobych or Buchach. The Austrian Society of Literature has placed a plaque by the main entrance to the gymnasium commemorating its most famous student, the author Joseph Roth (1894–1939), who studied there in 1905–13. While in the German he is described merely as a writer (*Dichter*), the Ukrainian text describes him as an "Austrian writer," which may seem ironic to those who know that he was born and raised as a Jew in Brody and eventually had to escape from Nazi Germany and Austria to Paris, where he died in a poorhouse.[156]

On the other side of the door we find a plaque to General Myron Tarnavs'kyi, who graduated there in 1889 and was the commander of the Ukrainian Galician Army in 1919, and above the door painted on a large sign is the ubiquitous portrait of Taras Shevchenko, who is depicted as urging his Ukrainian brothers to read and study. A new monument has recently been installed in front of the gymnasium, bearing the likenesses and names of Brody's famous sons (no daughters are mentioned). These young men include the painter Ivan Trush (1869–1941), the folklorist Osyp Rozdol's'kyi, the scholar and writer Vasyl' Shchurat (1871–1948), and the writer Stepan Tudor (1892–1941), as well as Roth, who appears last on the list (probably due to his year of birth) but is internationally far better known than the others.

Brody had been a center of Talmudic learning and Hasidism; the sages of the Brody "Kloiz" were known as the "lions and tigers in Torah and piety," and the town served for a while as the home of the founder of Hasidism, the Baal Shem Tov. It experienced a flowering of Hebrew and Yiddish literature, and served

---

[156] In this context see, e.g., Albert Lichtblau, ed., *Als hätten wir dazugehört: Österreichisch-jüdische Lebensgeschichten aus der Habsburgermonarchie* (Vienna: Boehlau, Leo Baeck Institute, Institute for History of Jews in Austria, 1999). In a wider sense, Roth was a writer of the multiethnic Austro-Hungarian Empire, and in a narrower sense he was a Jewish-Galician author. But like other cosmopolitan Jewish writers of that age, such as Stefan Zweig, there was no room for him in a nationalistic, racist, and anti-Semitic Austria-Germany, in which he could no longer be either Austrian or Jewish, and like Zweig, he lamented the world he had lost. Thus one can describe his novels, *The Radetzky March* and *The Emperor's Tomb* (as well as Zweig's *The World of Yesterday*) as sagas of the disintegration of the empire, while *The Wandering Jews* and *Job* are novels on the end of Galician Jewish civilization. See full citations in "Additional Readings."

as the launching pad for such founders of the Yiddish theater as the Broder Singers. No wonder that it was also known as "the Jerusalem of Austria." For students of Hebrew literature, one of its prominent sons was the literary critic and researcher Dov Sadan (1902–89), who also wrote a great deal about Brody in his memoirs.[157]

Among other tales, Sadan recounts the seemingly apocryphal story about the old Jewish cemetery, which was apparently destroyed by a Jew who had hoped to persuade the community to leave the Diaspora and return to the Land of Israel. That cemetery now serves as a soccer field behind the gymnasium. Ironically, the only other remnant of Jewish existence in Brody today is the "new cemetery," somewhat outside of town, a vast field of roughly 5,000 huge tombstones, some of them over six feet tall, many intricately inscribed and decorated, dating approximately between 1838 and 1938. This site, bordering a forest and a hill, from which the hull of the Great Synagogue can just be seen, is being gradually destroyed by an estimated 2,000 trees and bushes that are sprouting among the tombstones. Recently, thanks to initiatives by Ukrainian Jewish communities and American organizations, the cemetery has been surrounded by a fence, the stones have been photographed in order to record their inscriptions, and some clearing work has been initiated.[158]

At the edge of the field, on a small mound facing the cemetery, with its back to the forest in which many of the Jews were

[157] Dov Sadan, *From the Regions of Childhood* (Tel Aviv: Davar, 1938, in Hebrew).

[158] "International Notes," *Jewish Heritage Report*, no. 1 (March 1997). http://www.isjm.org/jhr/no1/int'l.htm (accessed December 3, 2006); "Brody Jewish Cemetery Restoration, Ukraine," *U.S. Commission for the Preservation of America's heritage Abroad*, http://www.heritageabroad.gov/projects/ukraine3.html (accessed December 3, 2006).

FIGURE 57. The "new" Jewish cemetery, Brody, 2004.

murdered, a simple monument has been erected. We climb up the few concrete stairs leading to a tombstone-like plaque bearing an inscription in Hebrew, Ukrainian, and English. The wording of the text indicates that it was written after the fall of Communism. The subtle differences between the three versions provide some insight into the divergent memories of the event. Thus the English inscription provides the standard commemorative statement: "In memory of the holy martyrs—Jews that were ruthlessly killed by the Nazi murderers." The Ukrainian text, for its part, makes an effort to include the Jewish victims in a Ukrainian memory of victimhood from which Jews have been largely excluded, even as this memory has also suppressed Ukrainian collaboration in the killings: "In memory of the

185

tormented [martyred] fellow-Jews cruelly annihilated by the Nazi murderers." And the Hebrew text is bitter, unforgiving, and closely based on the traditional formula of commemorating the victims of persecution: "This place is a common grave for the martyrs who were murdered for sanctifying God by the Nazis may their name be erased. May God avenge their blood." A basket of dry flowers placed in front of the memorial has been upset by the wind, which now rustles among the weeds grown as high as the tombstones. For a moment it seems as if the entire vast field of dark heavy stones and green and yellow weeds is swaying back and forth with the breeze, as pious Jews do when they pray. Then everything becomes still again.

Zhovkva / Żółkiew / Zsholkvo

FIGURE 58. The Great Synagogue, Zhovkva, 2003.

WE ARE about to complete our tour, now heading directly west to the town of Zhovkva, about 20 miles north of L'viv.[159] Built

[159] For background see *Pinkas Hakehillot*, 206–13. See also Nathan Michael Gelber and Y. Ben-Shem, *The Book of Żółkiew* (Jerusalem: Diaspora Encyclopedia, 1969, in Hebrew) scanned copy, http://yizkor.nypl.org/index.php?id=2312 (accessed December 3, 2006). Zhovkva city webpage and further information: "Zhovkva," http://www.geocities.com/zhovkva/zhovkva_e.html (accessed December 3, 2006); "The history of Zhovkva Town," http://www.geocities.com/zhovkva/history_e.html (accessed December 3, 2006); "Zhovkva Synagogue" http://www.babylon.com/definition/Zhovkva%20Synagogue/All (accessed December 3, 2006).

as a private fortress town in the late sixteenth century, the city suffered the fate of many other such border towns in the wars of the seventeenth century, coming under attacks by Tatars, Cossacks, Turks, Swedes, and Russians. To this day Zhovkva has an impressive castle that dates back to its founding, an early seventeenth-century Roman Catholic church in the Renaissance style, a Dominican convent built in the mid-seventeenth century (whose church has now been consecrated as Greek Catholic), a Basilian church and convent from the eighteenth century, and a magnificent synagogue completed in 1692. Built in late-Renaissance and baroque style, the synagogue was considered one of the most beautiful in Europe both for its unique exterior and for its sumptuous interior.

Uncharacteristically, a plaque attached to the synagogue provides basic details about its history, noting that the building was blown up by the Germans when they occupied the town, an act that destroyed its interior. Other versions, however, claim that the synagogue was torched during a pogrom by the local population. The plaque also indicates that in the mid-1950s some partial restoration was carried out on the roof and the façade of the synagogue, but that simultaneously the building was declared unusable. No mention is made of the fate of the community that had once used this edifice, nor of its fate. Since the 1950s the synagogue has been standing as an empty and deteriorating shell near the center of town, supported by rickety scaffolding and in a condition that suggests its approaching demise. This is in stark contradiction to the state of the other houses of worship, including the Roman Catholic Saint Lawrence Collegiate Church, which has been beautifully renovated since the fall of the Communist regime.[160]

---

[160] It is reported that the synagogue will be restored and will serve as a regional Jewish museum, and that funds have been allocated to that purpose by

Jews are known to have resided in Zhovkva since close to its establishment. By 1890 the nearly 4,000 Jewish inhabitants of the town constituted just over half the total population. Following World War I the city stagnated, and the Jewish population became impoverished. In 1931 there were some 4,400 Jews on Zhovkva, again about half the total population. In 1939 the city was flooded with Jewish refugees from German-occupied Poland, hundreds of whom were deported further east by the occupying Soviet authorities. Soon after the Germans marched in on June 28, 1941, and following the discovery of the bodies of prisoners murdered by the NKVD in the local prison, the Jewish population was subjected to a pogrom by local Ukrainians and Poles. It was at that point that the Great Synagogue is said to have been set on fire.

The first deportation took place in March 1942, when about 700 sick and elderly people were taken to Bełżec. Throughout summer 1942 numerous trains traveled via Zhovkva to Bełżec with Jews from other towns in Eastern Galicia. Many people on board these trains reportedly jumped out and tried to escape to the forest; but most were hunted down by the Germans, the Ukrainian guards, and the local population living along the railroad tracks in the Zhovkva region. A second *Aktion* took place in November, in which 2,000 Jews were concentrated in the yard of the castle, of whom about 300 were shot on the spot and the rest were deported to Bełżec. In March 1943 approximately 600 men were send to the Yaniv (Janowska) camp in

---

the World Monuments Fund, a private New York-based historic preservation organization, and by the Ukrainian government. But the project, if it is happening at all, is still in its early stages. See "Jewish Cemeteries, Synagogues, and mass Grave Sites in Ukraine," *United States Commission for the Preservation of America's Heritage*, 2005, http://www.heritageabroad.gov/reports/doc/survey_ukraine_2005.pdf (accessed December 3, 2006), 2, 21–22, 27, 62, 65–67, 76, 93, 136, 180.

FIGURE 59. The courtyard of the castle, Zhovkva, 2003.

L'viv, following which the ghetto was liquidated and whoever tried to escape was hunted down by the surrounding local population. Most of the remaining Jews were executed in the nearby forest. The last labor camp in town was liquidated in July 1943 and its forty inmates were also shot in the forest. All other Jews discovered in hiding later on were shot at the local Jewish cemetery. Only some seventy survivors came out of hiding following the liberation, after having been hunted down to the very end by Banderivtsi units active in and around Zhovkva.

One mass grave of Jews is located at the municipal cemetery in the center of town. The grave is neither marked nor protected. The main Jewish cemetery, still surrounded by a continuous masonry wall with a nonlocking gate, however, has been converted into an open-air market. The Germans had removed the tombstones and used them for paving roads. Other stones were incorporated into structures and utilized as repair material for the wall that surrounds the cemetery, either during the German occupation or subsequently. Gravestones that formerly belonged to the cemetery are said to have dated from as early as 1610. The cemetery also contains unmarked mass graves. Yet another mass grave is located in the forest east of Zhovkva, and is neither protected nor officially marked, although the site does contain discernible mass graves.[161] The day that I visited Zhovkva, on a Saturday afternoon in March 2003, the open-air market had just closed. The muddy field was strewn with garbage. A small structure had been erected next to the wall surrounding this large area as a "memorial tent" to commemorate former rabbis of the town. The rest of the field was taken up by half-buried vehicle tires marking out the path for commercial traffic and several large sheds.

Yet the memory of the Jews keeps haunting Zhovkva, and while it is connected to blood and suffering, it resurfaces in precisely the kind of distorted manner that must indicate the refusal of repressed memories to go away and of unresolved guilt to recede into the past. The town of Zhovkva does not, of course, display total amnesia. Indeed, at the center of town a

---

[161] "International Association of Jewish Genealogical Societies—Cemetery Project," http://www.jewishgen.org/cemetery/e-europe/ukra-z.html (accessed December 3, 2006); "Jewish Cemeteries," http://www.heritageabroad.gov/reports/doc/survey_ukraine_2005.pdf (accessed December 3, 2006), 41, 47, 49, 51, 112, 136, 179.

FIGURE 60. The Jewish cemetery in Zhovkva as open market, 2003.

memorial has been placed, which reminds the population of one episode in the past. It reads:

> In the years 1939–1941 Zhovkva Castle housed the district section of the NKVD—the main perpetrator of Stalinist repression in the territory of the region. It deported hundreds of Ukrainian and Polish families and imprisoned hundreds of Zhovkva residents, accusing them of disloyalty to Soviet power. On June 23–28, 1941, before the German forces seized Zhovkva, tragic events occurred within the walls of the fortress. Sadistic NKVD men tortured and executed the prisoners without trial or judgment . . . . Rotting in the rooms and in several concealed pits in the area of the castle, the mutilated bodies of the innocent victims of June 29, 1941 were sorrowfully buried.

This lamentation of the bitter fate of the Christian population of Zhovkva—clearly a legacy and symbol of the liberation from Communist subjugation—makes no mention of Jews, let alone of the complicity of the non-Jewish population in their mass murder. But because of this repression of a past that still stares one in the face, the recent discovery of a new mass grave in town was greeted not as an opportunity to face up to that deeply denied history but rather as a trigger for a new wave of prejudice and denial.

As Roman Woronowycz reported in the *Ukrainian Weekly* on September 29, 2002, about three months earlier the monks of the Zhovkva Basilian Monastery uncovered the remains of 228 bodies while remodeling the basement of their building. As it turned out, only eleven bodies appeared to have bullet holes in the skull, while another six seemed to have been struck on the head with sharp objects. No less than eighty-seven of the bodies belonged to children, two of whom were unborn. The local Memorial Society of L'viv, which publicized the discovery and collaborated in the investigation, swiftly came to the conclusion that these were victims of a Soviet massacre. According to Mr. Hryniv, president of the Memorial Society and a former member of Parliament, "This was the work of the NKVD; we have evidence to show that this is undeniable." To buttress his theory, Hryniv argued that Soviet newspaper clippings and coins found next to the bodies belonged to the postwar period.

Hryniv further commented that between 1946 and 1949 the Basilian monastery was used as a garrison by the NKVD, which was employed in the region to ferret out Ukrainian members and supporters of the UPA and the OUN, as well as Nazi collaborators and all other so-called "bourgeois nationalists." Hence he believed that the victims belonged to one of two categories of people. Either they were Ukrainians who had been ethnically cleansed by the Polish authorities in the notorious Operation Vistula and were executed by the NKVD after refusing to act as their spies,[162] or they were local people who had been targeted for deportation to Siberia but were discovered too late to be included in the transports and were therefore killed on the spot so as not to reveal the inefficiency of the secret police.

This elaborate theory was rejected out of hand, however, by the Kyiv journalist Danylo Kulyniak, who had written influential articles on the discovery in 1990 of Soviet mass killing sites near Ivano-Frankivs'k. To his mind the bodies found in Zhovkva had all the hallmarks of SS killings. As he put it: "How come the bodies are not clothed, and why no gold teeth were found?" Indeed, the bodies also had no hair, and no clasps, jewelry, or buttons were found at the site. Stating what much of the public in the West already knew, Kulyniak commented that the Germans took everything they could from their victims, whereas the Soviets were inclined to bury the bodies as they were, and rarely even stole gold teeth. He also

---

[162] Operation Vistula was actually part of a much larger exercise in ethnic cleansing and population transfers in the aftermath of World War II. Between 1945 and 1948, nearly 1.3 million Poles moved voluntarily or were forced from Volhynia and Eastern Galicia to Poland (as Poland's borders were moved to the west). Conversely, close to 500,000 Ukrainians and Lemkos (a Carpathian ethnic group associated by the authorities with the Ukrainians) were moved from Poland to the newly incorporated western regions of Soviet Ukraine. Continuing UPA actions provoked the Polish Communist government to unleash Operation Vistula, in which 140,000 Ukrainians and Lemkos living in the Carpathian region were forcibly deported to the western and northern regions of Poland (recently annexed from defeated Germany). Many UPA members either escaped to the west or crossed over the border to keep up the fight in Western Ukraine. See Magocsi, *History of Ukraine*, 642, 649; Snyder, *Reconstruction of Nations*, 187–201.

stressed that Soviet perpetrators did not normally murder women and children, certainly not on such a large scale. The usual practice was rather to take away the children of families perceived as a threat to the Soviet state and to place them in special schools.

Kulyniak thus concluded that the remains belonged to the local Jews of Zhovkva. He suggested that the Jews might have been killed in gas vans and then buried in the basement of the monastery. Another, and more likely, scenario he proposed was that following their occupation of the region, the Soviet authorities collected the remains of Jews eliminated by the Germans and buried them under the monastery as part of a clean-up operation. Interestingly for a man who was himself born in Zhovkva, Kulyniak hypothesized that the Soviets were keenly aware of the local population's inability to distinguish between Nazi and Soviet murders, and were therefore inclined to cover up the traces of German crimes as well as their own. Kulyniak suggested that most probably these were victims of epidemics, though his further notion that they were people in detention awaiting deportation to Siberia is far-fetched precisely because of the condition of the bodies he noted himself. Rather, it is possible that the Soviets collected bodies of Jews who died in epidemics in the ghetto and had already been robbed of their clothes and teeth, and buried them in the monastery partly for the reasons mentioned above and partly as a symbolic act of punishment and desecration of a specifically identified Ukrainian religious institution.

None of these arguments persuaded Mr. Hryniv of the Memorial Society. To his mind, in order for the truth to be discovered all possibilities had to be identified and considered and only then could final conclusions be drawn. As he put it: "These were not members of the underground, these were not combatants against the Soviet regime, they were not members of the

UPA or the OUN, these were mothers and children. And this is the best evidence that it was a war against the civilian population."[163] Clearly, Hryniv's theory is untenable and contradicts everything we know about Nazi and Soviet killing methods and the realities on the ground in Eastern Galicia. Why then his insistence on this harebrained idea? In part, this obviously has to do with the desire to blame all evil deeds on the Soviets, not difficult to understand after close to half a century of oppression, especially from the perspective of a Ukrainian nationalist. But there is more at play here, which has to do not just with identifying the victims, but also with transforming them into perpetrators. To be sure, this is not mentioned explicitly by Hryniv. But glancing at some more extreme responses to the discovery of the mass grave at Zhovkva sheds a painful light on the long-term effects of repression. For while not a few Jewish survivors from these regions—as well as many other observers and commentators at the time and since the Holocaust—have maintained that "the Ukrainians were worse than the Germans," the line of defense taken up by Ukrainian nationalists who identify with the UPA and OUN of World War II and with their

[163] Roman Woronowycz, "Mass Grave at Zhovkva Monastery: The Mystery Continues," *Ukrainian Weekly*, September 29, 2002, http://www.ukrweekly.com/ Archive/2002/390204.shtml (accessed December 3, 2006). For an earlier report see Roman Woronowycz, "Soviet-era mass grave unearthed in western Ukraine," *Ukrainian Weekly*, July 28, 2002, http://www.ukrweekly.com/Archive/ 2002/300201.shtml (accessed December 3, 2006). This story was also reported in the United States though it did not receive much coverage. See Peter Baker, "Soviet-Era Atrocity Unearthed in Ukraine: Remains of 225 Apparently Killed by Secret Police Are Found at Monastery," *Washington Post*, July 23, 2002, A1, http://www.artukraine.com/events/atrocity.htm (accessed December 3, 2006). See also "Mass Grave Found at Ukrainian Monastery," *BBC News*, July 16, 2002, http://news.bbc.co.uk/1/hi/world/europe/2131954.stm (accessed December 3, 2006).

anti-Semitic policies is that the "Soviets, led by the Jews, were worse than the Germans."[164]

[164] See, e.g., "Israel Asper: Sixth Explanation of Israeli Barbarism," mail archive, http://www.mail-archive.com/antinato@topica.com/msg06933.html (accessed December 3, 2006); "Holocaust History Archive," http://litek.ws/k0nsl/detox/Carto-nine-reasons.html (accessed December 3, 2006). According to Redlich, "Metropolitan Andrei Sheptyts'kyi," while Sheptyts'kyi initially welcomed the Germans because they drove out the Soviets, he eventually concluded that they were worse than the Soviets. It has meanwhile been reported in the October 25, 2006 Internet issue of *ForUm*, "NKVD Victims to Be Buried in Lviv on November 7," http://en.for-ua.com/news/2006/10/25/171101.html (accessed December 3, 2006), that the L'viv City Council Executive Committee decided "to bury the remains of NKVD victims at Lychakivsky cemetery." The "approximately 500 people" are described by *ForUm* as "victims of the repressions of the 1940s" whose "human remains were all found in the Zhovka [*sic*] district of the Lviv region." The report goes on to say that the "burial will take place in the memorial seventy sixth Crypt of the Cemetery," and that the "Lviv Regional State Administration plans to create an Avenue of Honoured Graves at the Lychakivsky Cemetery by the end of 2006," which is intended also to accommodate "the remains of the leaders of the Organization of Ukrainian Nationalists Yevhen Konovalets, Stepan Bandera, Andriy Melnyk and other leaders of the national liberation struggle." A "public committee" established in 2002 in L'viv has been charged with the task of bringing back the bodies of Bandera, who is buried in Munich, and of Konovalets, who is buried in Rotterdam. Thanks to Delphine Bechtel for drawing my attention to this development.

III

RETURN

For ultimately, this is not only a story about exhuming bodies, but also about unearthing a past of destruction whose very objective was to bury the traces of its crimes and the identity of the murdered along with their bodies. But such crimes have a predilection to resurface, both metaphorically and physically. They cannot remain hidden forever, and they cannot be confronted without a willingness to look back at all the hatred and atrocity, but also the beauty and creativity, of a world that ended up being trampled by vast external forces even as it devoured its own inhabitants. Those who stare at that past with eyes wide shut can only conjure fictions, legends, nightmares, and phobias, however much they seek a pure, good, cleansed identity.

We cannot bring back the dead, but we can give them a decent burial. We cannot bring back a rich, complex, and increasingly precarious multiethnic world, and we may not even want to do so, but we can recognize its failings and respect its accomplishments, not only for their own sake, but because we cannot understand ourselves and build a secure and confident identity without acknowledging where we come from and how we got to where we are today. We have just left behind us the bloodiest century in world history, and seem to be heading right into one that could prove to be even bloodier. Before we plunge into yet another ocean of blood, it behooves us to reflect on the causes and consequences of previous atrocities and to finally understand that the origins of collective violence invariably lie in repressing memory and misconstruing the past.

Some nations have looked back at the horrors of the past—
those of their own doing and those that have been perpetrated
upon them—with greater willingness and success than others.
There is a common, perhaps a natural, predilection to contemplate one's own suffering with greater empathy than that of
others. It becomes all the more difficult to empathize with
the victimhood of others if this victimhood was fully or even
partially caused by one's own actions; in such cases, the more
emphasis is put on our pain and loss, the less necessary it seems
to remember those whom we have harmed. Indeed, there is a
certain tendency to invert the link between what was done to us
and what we did to others, in a manner that not only ignores
the suffering of our victims but makes them responsible both
for our misfortune and for their own destruction. Finally, since
we are speaking here of collective, national, and ideological
narratives and representations, there is also the often distorted
connection between glory, heroism, and martyrdom, on the
one hand, and betrayal, treason, and criminality on the other.
In this kind of polarity it all too often appears that one's own
national honor can be salvaged only by besmirching the nation,
culture, or religion of those whom one wronged. This is the
process by which a vicious cycle of defining enemies and making victims is created.[1]

Germany, to which Albert Einstein once referred as "a country of mass murderers," has struggled mightily with the legacy
of genocide.[2] It has become almost a cliché to say that postwar
Germans have "come to terms with the past," or, indeed, have
"overcome" it. If there was ever any single nation that by its
massive support for a criminal regime bears responsibility for

[1] Omer Bartov, *Mirrors of Destruction: War, Genocide, and Modern Identity*
(New York: Oxford University Press, 2000), chap. 3.

[2] In a letter to Max Born, dated October 12, 1953, cited in Fritz Stern,
Einstein's German World (Princeton: Princeton University Press, 1999), 3.

the crimes committed in its name and by its members, this was the German nation under Hitler's rule. Yet even in this case the arguments have never actually ceased. Were the Germans Hitler's "willing executioners" or his victims?[3] Has Germany spoken enough about its own crimes and should it now "finally" turn its attention to its own suffering?[4] Has Germany in fact "overcome" the past, or is it chained to it, enslaved to a memory of atrocity that will not let it look to a better future? When can it be liberated from Auschwitz and who has the right to set it free?

None of these dilemmas have simple or easy solutions. But despite a great deal of resistance, anger, and resentment in some circles, they are perceived in Germany as crucial issues that must be, and are, confronted on a daily basis. Germany may be ready again to remember the suffering of Germans in a war they brought upon themselves, but it has also recently completed the construction of a vast memorial to its victims on one of the most desirable pieces of real estate in Europe, right next to the symbols and centers of German power. Precisely this recognition of guilt and responsibility has made it easier for Germans and others to accept and even to take pleasure in that nation's reunification and return to the center of world politics, economic prosperity, and cultural exuberance.[5]

France also struggled with the memory of war, defeat, and occupation. After several decades of acquiescing to the "myth of

[3] Daniel Jonah Goldhagen, *Hitler's Willing Executioners: Ordinary Germans and the Holocaust* (New York: Knopf, 1996).

[4] W. G. Sebald, *On the Natural History of Destruction*, trans. Anthea Bell (New York: Random House, 2003), esp. the essay "Air War and Literature," 1–104; Jörg Friedrich, *Der Brand: Deutschland im Bombenkrieg 1940–1945* (Berlin: Propyläen, 2002).

[5] On Berlin's current culture of memory, see Karen E. Till, *The New Berlin: Memory, Politics, Place* (Minneapolis: University of Minnesota Press, 2005).

the Resistance" articulated by Charles de Gaulle, the French were compelled to contemplate a far-less-edifying past of collaboration with their German occupiers and widespread governmental and administrative support for the deportation of the country's Jews to Nazi extermination camps. If in the early postwar years France's Jewish victims were incorporated into the myth of the Resistance, since the 1980s their unique fate has been increasingly recognized.[6] Yet it took until the administration of Jacques Chirac for the French state to officially recognize its responsibility for the crimes of Vichy. And the competition of memories and victimhood, between the heroism of the Resistance and the mass murder of the Jews, and the repercussions of these different historical narratives on the identity of contemporary French men and women, including several hundred thousand Jews and several million Muslims, are all still very much part of public debate in France. Still, the most painful aspects of that ambivalent past have been faced and confronted. If France today is having difficulties in solving its present problems, this is not because of any major failure to look critically back at its past.

More akin to Ukraine is the case of Poland. In France there had been a tendency in the early postwar years to incorporate the Jewish victims of the Holocaust within the general narrative of the "deportees"—who were understood as members of the Resistance and thus as representatives of the *Grande Nation*. In Poland the Jewish victims were incorporated into the general

---

[6] The most important contributions to shifting French historical thinking about the Occupation were Robert O. Paxton, *Vichy France: Old Guard and New Order, 1940–1944* (New York: Knopf, 1972); Henry Rousso, *The Vichy Syndrome: History and Memory in France since 1944*, trans. Arthur Goldhammer (1987; Cambridge, Mass.: Harvard University Press, 1991); Annette Wieviorka, *Déportation et génocide: Entre la mémoire et l'oubli* (Paris: Plon, 1992); and the film by Marcel Ophuls, *The Sorrow and the Pity* (1969).

narrative of Polish victimhood even as Jews were still seen to some degree as instigators of that very same victimhood. It was common to assert in Poland for many years that just as there were six million Jewish victims in the Holocaust, so too there were six million Polish victims in the war. Hence both nations had a Holocaust and shared a similar fate, although Polish narratives of the past glorified their nation's martyrdom as one of active resistance to the Nazi invaders, while perceiving the Jews more as passive victims. In fact, of course, of the six million Polish victims, three million were Catholic or ethnic Poles, and three million were Jewish citizens of Poland. Moreover, even as Poland did courageously resist the German occupation and paid a horrendous price for its struggle, numerous Polish patriots and nationalists were also anything but displeased with the "removal" of the Jews from their country, and not a few collaborated in the effort to bring about that "removal." Admitting collaboration with or at least approval of Nazi crimes obviously compromised both the Polish narrative of glorious resistance and the historical self-definition of Poland as "the Christ of nations," the eternal martyr.

Unlike West Germany and France, Poland was under Communist rule, and much of the discourse on the past was determined by a mixture of ideological dictates with local national traditions and sensibilities. Many Poles continued to identify Jews with Communism, and Communism with the occupation of their land by the Soviets, who were seen as not much better than the Germans. Polish Communist regimes in fact also conducted blatant anti-Semitic policies that were in stark contradiction to the utter discrediting of anti-Semitic rhetoric in respectable political circles in the West. This too made coming to terms with the past very difficult. It took a few courageous local scholars and intellectuals, and some who were living outside the country, to finally shake up the consensus and make "the poor Poles look at the ghetto."[7] Perhaps the best indication of how different national memories of the same event can be was the reaction to the publication of Jan Gross's book on the massacre of the Jews of Jedwabne by their Polish neighbors.[8] In Poland the book was greeted with astonishment, since the general view had been that the Germans were completely responsible for the Holocaust, and therefore it had nothing to do with Polish conduct. In Israel the book was seen as merely affirming what many had long believed, namely, that the Poles were both pleased with and often participated in the murder of their Jewish co-citizens.

The struggle with the past has not ended in Poland. Recent writings and pronouncements seem to indicate that the myth of the *Żydokomuna* (Jews as communists) has not gone away. Some younger Polish scholars claim again that the nation's Jewish citizens were disloyal to it during the Soviet occupation and therefore had to be suppressed by the forces of the state. The right-wing turn in Polish politics is thus reflected also in reconstructions of the past.[9] Still, Poland has gone a long

---

[7] I am referring here, of course, to Jan Błoński, "The Poor Poles Look at the Ghetto," in Polonsky, *My Brother's Keeper?*, 34–48. The essay was originally published in the journal *Tygodnik Powszechny* on January 11, 1987. On this see also Zimmerman, *Contested Memories*; and the differing positions in the following: Gunnar S. Paulsson, *Secret City: The Hidden Jews of Warsaw, 1940–1945* (New Haven: Yale University Press, 2002); Leo Cooper, *In the Shadow of the Polish Eagle: The Poles, the Holocaust and Beyond* (New York: Palgrave, 2000); Richard C. Lukas, *Forgotten Holocaust: The Poles under German Occupation, 1939–1944*, 2nd rev. ed. (New York: Hippocrene Books, 1997).

[8] Gross, *Neighbors*.

[9] See Chodakiewicz, *After the Holocaust*; Marek Wierzbicki, *Polacy i Żydzi w zaborze sowieckim: Stosunki polsko-żydowskie na ziemiach północno-wschodnich II RP pod okupacją sowiecką (1939–1941)* (Warsaw: Stowarzyszenie Kulturalne Fronda, 2001).

way since the time of the Kielce Pogrom and the Gomułka regime.[10] In many Polish cities and towns the remnants of Jewish civilization are being preserved, even celebrated. It has become almost chic for younger Poles to claim some Jewish ancestry or at least to show an interest in the Jewish past of Polish civilization. When my old friend Ilona Karmel visited her hometown of Cracow in the 1970s, she said that it looked exactly as she remembered it from prewar times, but that all the people seemed to have been taking their siesta. Nowadays the former Jewish quarter of Kazimierz is positively hopping, and one can eat "Jewish" food, complete with menus in Hebrew (which the local waiters cannot even read) and surrounded by "Jewish" bric-a-brac picked up at the flea market. There is an aspect of cheap commercialization and faddish, questionable taste in all this, of course. But the bottom line is that Poland is willing, indeed at times seemingly eager to adopt its Jewish past, a past of a once multiethnic, multidenominational society which lasted for many centuries before the wars and ideologies of the twentieth century obliterated it and most of its traces.[11]

---

[10] Jan T. Gross, *Fear: Anti-Semitism in Poland after Auschwitz: An Essay in Historical Interpretation* (New York: Random House, 2006); Daniel Blatman, "Polish Jewry, the Six-Day War, and the Crisis of 1968," in *The Six-Day War and World Jewry*, ed. Eli Lederhendler (Bethesda: University Press of Maryland, 2000), 291–310; Bożena Szaynok, "The Role of Antisemitism in Postwar Polish-Jewish Relations," and Dariusz Stola, "Fighting against the Shadows: The *Anti-Zionist* Campaign of 1968," both in *Antisemitism and Its Opponents in Modern Poland,* ed. Robert Blobaum (Ithaca: Cornell University Press, 2005), 265–83 and 284–300, respectively.

[11] One important Polish organization deeply involved in resurrecting the multicultural past of Poland's borderlands is Krzysztof Czyżewski's Pogranicze Foundation and publishing house in Sejny. For more information, see "Borderland Archipelago, http://www.pogranicze.sejny.pl/ (accessed December 3, 2006).

This is still not happening in Ukraine, certainly not in the Western Ukrainian lands of the former Eastern Galicia. How then does one explain the almost aggressive urge to push out of memory and hide from sight, to demolish or desecrate all remaining traces of Jewish life and civilization there? Why is there such a powerful desire to blatantly fill spaces that were sites of Jewish life and death with symbols of Ukrainian nationalism and glory? There clearly cannot be a single explanation for this phenomenon. In part, I believe, it has to do with the fact that Ukraine is only gradually and haltingly emerging from a troubled past; as recent political events there indicate, it is still not certain about its own national identity, and therefore its past becomes an important site of contestation between different interpretations of where Ukraine belongs and to whom. Tragically, both right-wing Ukrainian nationalists, who want to distance it from Russia and the Soviet past, and former Soviet apparatchiks, who want to remain part of the Russian sphere, agree on the need to make as little as possible of the unique fate of Ukrainian Jewry during the war.

But the nationalists of Galicia go much farther than that. For in this region the memory of the OUN and the UPA is a crucial component in the creation of a Ukrainian and a local sense of identity, of glory, and of heroism, which was deeply suppressed under Communist rule (as was the memory of Jewish victimhood). But once these nationalist organizations are given back their place of honor in history, one cannot possibly associate them with collaboration in the murder of the Jews. Moreover, by adopting the OUN and UPA as symbols of Galician nationalism, one must to some extent also adopt what they actually stood for, which was, after all, Ukraine for the Ukrainians and cleansing the land of such "foreign elements" as the Jews and the Poles. From this perspective it is "natural" to put a statue of Bandera on the grounds of the Drohobych ghetto, because his legacy has indeed finally won, and the Soviets, the Poles, the Germans, and the Jews are gone forever.

Clearly this also means that another legacy is still very present particularly in these western regions of Ukraine, namely, anti-Semitism. This is a notoriously difficult sentiment to gage, as are its intensity and implications. For many Galicians, it seems, Jews remain associated both with past suffering under the Soviets and with the ills of the Kuchma regime. Deeper historical memories associate the Jews with the exploiters of Ukrainian peasants, with wealth and arrogance and collaboration with foreign rulers.[12] Among some circles, these images are now intermingled with the new anti-Semitism that presents Israel as the continuation of Jewish exploitation and power and Jews as the proxies of such evil empires as the United States, this time also spreading their malign influence in the Middle East. The deep and rotten roots of anti-Semitism, a disease that makes it impossible for individuals and whole societies to

[12] In this context one could also contemplate the implications of the following passage by the American-Ukrainian historian Taras Hunczak, written before the fall of Communism, on Jewish complicity in Soviet crimes and Ukrainian complicity in Nazi crimes: "To date . . . there is no thorough study of this important and highly complex question, and it is therefore impossible to render a final judgment about the nature of Jewish and Ukrainian behavior during World War II. It would be just as outrageous to suggest that the Jewish people as a whole are responsible for the criminal acts perpetrated against Ukrainians by Jews who actively supported the Soviets, as it would be to maintain that Ukrainians as a whole are accountable for the anti-Semitic actions of a few." See Taras Hunczak, "Ukrainian-Jewish Relations during the Soviet and Nazi Occupations," in *Ukraine during World War II: History and its Aftermath*, ed. Yury Boshyk (Edmonton: University of Alberta, 1986), 43–44. While Hunczak is obviously keen to dismantle mutual Jewish and Ukrainian prejudices about each other, the entirely false equivalence he proposes between Ukrainian and Jewish complicity (collective or otherwise) in perpetrating crimes on each other merely betrays the fact that he is subjected to precisely those prejudices he wishes to expose.

examine themselves by repeatedly stating that "the Jews are our misfortune," have still not been exposed to the sunlight in these parts of Western Ukraine.

But it is only by exposing these roots and uncovering the hidden past that Eastern Galicia will be able to recover its rich, complex, tumultuous, yet also extraordinarily creative past. It is a beautiful land, rich in cultural resources, history, and future potential. Once it liberates itself from the stranglehold of a distorted and semiconcealed past and recovers the true tragedy as well as the full glory of its history, it will be able, once more, to become the bridge between West and East, the borderland of communication and exchange that it once was, rather than remaining a forgotten patch of territory on the edge of Europe, out of time and out of sight.[13]

---

[13] There are two other ways in which Galicia is remembered both as a reality and as an extinct entity. One is in the Jewish memorial books (and some similar Polish memorial books and journals) cited earlier. These books reflect the living memories of a generation that has almost vanished completely and therefore can serve from now on as a historical resource, though one that needs to be handled with care. See also Jack Kugelmass and Jonathan Boyarin, eds., *From a Ruined Garden: The Memorial Books of Polish Jewry*, 2nd ed. (Bloomington: Indiana University Press, 1998). What remains of these memories is the predilection of some descendents to speak of their ancestors' towns in Galicia (or elsewhere in Eastern Europe) as no longer being there, since having lost their Jewish population, they were deemed extinct by the few Jewish survivors who could only remember them as shtetlach. The other vicarious memory of these towns is that of the Hasidic dynasties that still carry the name of their rabbis from towns that have no recollection of these communities. Occasionally the disciples of these rabbis return to their towns, but they too do not perceive them as living entities and are often also not interested in the past of the Jewish communities there as a whole, but only in the "rebbe" who once resided there, for whom they may build a "memorial tent," a stone structure over his tombstone as a commemoration and mourning site. There are relatively small Hasidic dynasties or traditions for seven of the twenty towns described in this book: Chortkov (Chortkiv), Drohovitch (Drohobych),

Husiyatan (Husiatyn), Kosov (Kosiv), Sambur (Sambir), Stanislav (Ivano-Frankivs'k), and Zlotchov (Zolochiv). On the Chortkov Hasidic dynasty see *wikipedia*, S.V. "Chortkov Hasidic Dynasty," http://en.wikipedia.org/wiki/Chortkov_%28Hasidic_dynasty%29 (accessed December 3, 2006); and especially Abraham Heshel, "The Chasidic Group of Czortków," http://www.shtetlinks.jewishgen.org/Suchostaw/sl_czortkow_chasidic_group.htm (accessed December 3, 2006).

ACKNOWLEDGMENTS

Numerous friends and colleagues have helped me over the years with this book and my ongoing project on Buchach. I would like especially to thank the following for their generous help and constructive comments: Delphine Bechtel, Marco Carynnyk, Sofia Grachova, Jan Gross, Frank Grelka, Oleg Majewski, Joanna Michlic, Robert Moeller, Norman Naimark, Naama Shik, Tim Snyder, Amir Weiner, and Larry Wolff.

I am also grateful to the Radcliffe Institute for Advanced Study at Harvard, the Internationales Forschungszentrum Kulturwissenschaften (IFK) in Vienna, Austria, the John Simon Guggenheim Memorial Foundation, the American Academy in Berlin, and Brown University, for facilitating my research and writing.

For inspiration, empathy, support, and love, special thanks to my better half, Wai-yee Li, our children Shira and Rom, my son Raz, and my father Hanoch Bartov. If rumor has it right and we go somewhere after our demise, I hope that Ilona and my mother are there together, casting a kind if critical gaze at those who love and miss them.

• • • • •

Unless otherwise indicated, all photographs were taken by Omer Bartov ©.

ADDITIONAL READINGS

THE LITERATURE on the issues discussed in this book is vast, and it is obviously impossible to mention more than a fraction of it. Along with works cited in the notes, the reader may profit from consulting the following selection of studies and works of fiction:

Eastern Europe's Borderlands

"Borderlands: Ethnicity, Identity, and Violence in the Shatter-Zone of Empires Since 1848." Research project led by Omer Bartov at the Watson Institute for International Studies, Brown University, http://www.watsoninstitute.org/borderlands/, for numerous papers and links to other projects on this issue.

Bugge, Peter. "'Shatter Zones': The Creation and Re-Creation of Europe's East." In *Ideas of Europe since 1914: The Legacy of the First World War*, ed. Menno Spiering and Michael Wintle, 47–69. New York: Palgrave, 2002.

Wolff, Larry. *Inventing Eastern Europe: The Map of Civilization on the Mind of the Enlightenment.* Stanford: Stanford University Press, 1994.

Galicia

Bachmann, Klaus. *Ein Herd der Feindschaft gegen Rußland: Galizien als Krisenherd in den Beziehungen der Donaumonarchie mit Rußland (1907–1914).* Vienna: Verlag für Geschichte und Politik, 2001.

Hann, Christopher, and Paul Robert Magocsi, eds. *Galicia: A Multi-cultured Land.* Toronto: University of Toronto Press, 2005.

Markovits, Andrei S. and Frank E. Sysyn, eds. *Nationbuilding and the Politics of Nationalism: Essays on Austrian Galicia.* Cambridge, Mass.: Harvard University Press, 1982.

Ukrainian History and Nationalism

Fedyshyn, Oleh S. *Germany's Drive to the East and the Ukrainian Revolution, 1917–1918.* New Brunswick, N.J.: Rutgers University Press, 1971.

Himka, John-Paul. *Galician Villagers and the Ukrainian National Movement in the Nineteenth Century.* London: Macmillan, 1988.

———. *Religion and Nationality in Western Ukraine: The Greek Catholic Church and the Ruthenian National Movement in Galicia, 1867–1900.* Montreal: McGill-Queen's University Press, 1999.

Hrycak, Jarosław (Yaroslav Hrytsak). *Historia Ukrainy, 1772–1999: Narodziny nowoczesnego narodu.* Trans. Katarzyna Kotyńska. Lublin: Instytut Europy Środkowo-Wschodniej, 2000.

Hunczak, Taras, ed. *The Ukraine, 1917–1921: A Study in Revolution.* Cambridge, Mass.: Harvard University Press, 1977.

Kozik, Jan. *The Ukrainian National Movement in Galicia, 1815–1849.* Ed. Lawrence D. Orton. Trans. Andrew Gorski and Lawrence D. Orton. Toronto: University of Toronto Press, 1986.

Magocsi, Paul Robert. *The Roots of Ukrainian Nationalism: Galicia as Ukraine's Piedmont.* Toronto: Toronto University Press, 2002.

Ukrainian-Jewish Relations and Collaboration in the Holocaust

Berkhoff, Karel C. *Harvest of Despair: Life and Death in Ukraine Under Nazi Rule.* Cambridge, Mass.: Harvard University Press, 2004, esp. 59–88.

Dean, Martin. *Collaboration in the Holocaust: Crimes of the Local Police in Belorussia and Ukraine, 1941–44.* New York: St. Martin's Press, 2000.

Golczewski, Frank. "Interethnic Relations, Politics, and the Holocaust: Ukrainians, Germans, and Jews in Western Ukraine." In *The Shoah in Ukraine: History, Testimony, and Memorialization,* ed. Wendy Lower and Ray Brandon. Bloomington: Indiana University Press, 2007.

———. "Die Kollaboration in der Ukraine." In *Kooperation und Verbrechen: Formen der "Kollaboration" im östlichen Europa 1939–1945,* ed. Christoph Dieckmann et al., 151–82. Göttingen: Wallstein, 2003.

Himka, John-Paul. "Ukrainian Collaboration in the Extermination of the Jews During the Second World War: Sorting Out the Long-Term and Conjunctural Factors." In *The Fate of the European Jews, 1939–1945: Continuity or Contingency?* ed. Jonathan Frankel, 170–89. New York: Oxford University Press, 1997, and at http://www.zwoje-scrolls.com/zwoje16/text11p.htm.

———. "Ukrainian-Jewish Antagonism in the Galician Countryside during the Late Nineteenth Century." In *Ukrainian-Jewish Relations in Historical Perspective,* ed. Peter J. Potichnyj and Howard Aster, 111–58. Edmonton: University of Alberta, 1988.

Pohl, Dieter. "Ukrainische Hilfskräfte beim Mord an den Juden." In *Die Täter der Shoah: Fanatische Nationalsozialisten oder ganz normale Deutsche?* ed. Gerhard Paul, 205–34. Göttingen: Wallstein, 2002.

Sabrin, B. F. *Alliance for Murder: The Nazi-Ukrainian Nationalist Partnership in Genocide.* New York: Sarpedon, 1991.

Spector, Shmuel. *The Holocaust of Volhynian Jews, 1941–1944.* Trans. Jerzy Michalowicz. Jerusalem: Yad Vashem, 1990.

Torzecki, Ryszard. "Die Rolle der Zusammenarbeit mit der deutschen Besatzungsmacht in der Ukraine für deren Okkupationspolitik." In *Okkupation und Kollaboration (1938–1945). Beiträge zu Konzepten und Praxis der Kollaboration in der deutschen Okkupationspolitik,* ed. Werner Röhr, 239–72. Berlin: Hüthig, 1994.

Weiss, Aharon. "Jewish-Ukrainian Relations in Western Ukraine During the Holocaust." In *Ukrainian-Jewish Relations in Historical Perspective*, ed. Peter J. Potichnyj and Howard Aster, 409–420. Edmonton: University of Alberta, 1988.

Polish History and Nationalism

Dabrowski, Patrice M. *Commemorations and the Shaping of Modern Poland*. Bloomington: Indiana University Press, 2004.

Davies, Norman. *God's Playground: A History of Poland*. Rev. ed. 2 vols. New York: Oxford University Press, 2005.

Lukowski, Jerzy, and Hubert Zawadzki. *A Concise History of Poland*. Cambridge: Cambridge University Press, 2001.

Stauter-Halsted, Keely. *The Nation in the Village: The Genesis of Peasant National Identity in Austrian Poland, 1848–1948*. Ithaca: Cornell University Press, 2001.

Zamoyski, Adam. *The Polish Way: A Thousand-Year History of the Poles and Their Culture*. New York: Hippocrene Books, 1994.

Polish Romantic Literature

Milosz, Czeslaw. *The History of Polish Literature*. 2nd ed. Berkeley: University of California Press, 1983, esp. pts. 7–10.

Sienkiewicz, Henryk. *With Fire and Sword*. Trans. W. S. Kuniczak. New York: Hippocrene Books, 1991. First published in Polish in 1884; part 1 of trilogy.

———. *The Deluge*. Trans. W. S. Kuniczak. New York: Hippocrene Books, 1991. First published in Polish in 1886; part 2 of trilogy.

———. *Pan Michael*. Trans. Jeremiah Curtin. Boston: Little Brown, 1893. First published in Polish in 1887–88; part 3 of trilogy.

Ethnic Germans as Collaborators and Victims

Bergen, Doris L. "The Volksdeutsche of Eastern Europe and the Collapse of the Nazi Empire, 1944–1945." In *The Impact of Nazism: New Perspectives on the Third Reich and Its Legacy*, ed. Alan E. Steinwies and Daniel E. Rogers, 101–28. Lincoln: University of Nebraska Press, 2003.

Buchsweiler, Meir. *Russlanddeutsche im Sowjetsystem bis zum Zweiten Weltkrieg: Minderheitenpoltik, nationale Identität, Publizistik.* Essen: Klartext Verlag, 1995.

Dean, Martin. "The Role of Soviet Ethnic Germans in the Holocaust in the Reich Commissariat Ukraine." In Lower and Brandon, *Shoah in Ukraine,* chap. 7.

Lower, Wendy. *Nazi Empire-Building and the Holocaust in Ukraine.* Chapel Hill: University of North Carolina Press, 2005.

Lumans, Valdis O. "A Reassessment of *Volksdeutsche* and Jews in the Volhynia-Galicia-Narew Resettlement." In Steinwies and Rogers, *Impact of Nazism,* 81–100.

Röskau-Rydel, Isabel, ed. *Deutsche Geschichte im Osten Europas: Galizien.* Berlin: Siedler Verlag, 1999.

Polish and Galician Jewry

Abramsky, Chimen, et al., eds. *The Jews of Poland.* New York: Basil Blackwell, 1988.

Babicki, Jakov. *Yiddishe Landvitshaft in Stanislover Voiyevodshaft.* Wilno: Bibliotek fun YIVO, 1938, in Yiddish.

The Galitzianer. Newsletter of "Gesher Galicia," http://www.jew ishgen.org/galicia/newsletter.html.

Hödl, Klaus. *Als Bettler in die Leopoldstadt: Galizische Juden auf dem Weg nach Wien.* Vienna: Böhlau, 1994.

Hundert, Gershon David, ed. *Essential Papers on Hasidism: Origins to Present.* New York: New York University Press, 1991.

———. *The Jews in a Polish Private Town: The Case of Opatów in the Eighteenth Century*. Baltimore: Johns Hopkins University Press, 1992.

Lehmann, Rosa. *Symbiosis and Ambivalence: Poles and Jews in a Small Galician Town*. New York: Berghahn Books, 2001.

Mahler, Raphael. *Hasidism and the Jewish Enlightenment: Their Confrontation in Galicia and Poland in the First Half of the Nineteenth Century*. Philadelphia: Jewish Publication Society of America, 1985.

Moore, Deborah Dash, ed. *East European Jews in Two World Wars: Studies from the YIVO Annual*. Evanston: Northwestern University Press, 1990.

Shanes, Joshua. "National Regeneration in the Diaspora: Zionism, Politics and Jewish Identity in Late Habsburg Galicia, 1883–1907." Ph.D. diss., University of Wisconsin, 2002.

———. "Neither Germans nor Poles: Jewish Nationalism in Galicia before Herzl, 1883–1897." *Austrian History Yearbook* 34 (2003): 191–213.

Sinkoff, Nancy. *Out of the Shtetl: Making Jews Modern in the Polish Borderlands*. Providence: Brown University Judaic Studies, 2004.

Jewish Art and Literature

Agnon, Shmuel Yosef. *The Bridal Canopy*. Trans. I. M. Lask. New York: Schocken Books, 1967. Orig. pub. 1922.

———. *Das Buch von den polnischen Juden*. Berlin: Jüdischer Verlag, 1916.

———. *Buchach, moie rodynne misto* [My Hometown]. Ternopil': Erudyt, 2002. Ukrainian translation of a selection of his stories.

———. *A Guest for the Night: A Novel*. Trans. Misha Louvis. Madison: University of Wisconsin Press, 2004. Orig. pub. 1939.

———. *Only Yesterday*. Trans. Barbara Harshav. Princeton: Princeton University Press, 2000. Orig. pub. 1945.

———. *The Whole City*. Jerusalem: Schocken, 1973, in Hebrew.

Franzos, Karl Emil. *The Jews of Barnow.* Trans. M. W. Macdowall. North Stratford, N.H.: Ayer Company Publishers, 1999. Orig. pub. 1877.

———. *Leib Weihnachtskuchen and his Child.* Trans. Michael Mitchell. Riverside, Calif.: Adriane Press, 2005. Orig. pub. 1896.

Grynberg, Henryk. *Drohobycz, Drohobycz and Other Stories: True Tales from the Holocaust and Life After.* Trans. Alicia Nitecki. Ed. Theodosia Robertson. New York: Penguin Books, 2002.

Mendelsohn, Ezra. *Painting a People: Maurycy Gottlieb and Jewish Art.* Hanover, N.H.: University Press of New England, 2002.

Roth, Joseph. *The Emperor's Tomb.* Trans. John Hoare. Woodstock, N.Y.: Overlook Press, 2002. Orig. pub. 1938.

———. *Job.* Trans. Dorothy Thompson. Woodstock, N.Y.: Overlook Press, 2003. Orig. pub. 1930.

———. *The Radetzky March.* Trans. Joachim Neugroschel. Woodstock, N.Y.: Overlook Press, 2002. Orig. pub. 1932.

———. *The Wandering Jews.* Trans. Michael Hofmann. New York: W. W. Norton, 2001. Orig. pub. 1927.

Zweig, Stefan. *The World of Yesterday: An Autobiography.* Trans. Cedar and Eden Paul. London: Cassell, 1987. Orig. pub. 1944.

Holocaust Memoirs

Anderman, Pesach. *The Strength of Life: Being Human.* Ramat Gan: Te'omim, 2004, in Hebrew, on Buchach.

Appleman-Jurman, Alicia. *Alicia: My Story.* Toronto: Bantam Books, 1988, on Buchach.

Arbiser, Pola. *Give Me the Children.* Atlanta: William Breman Jewish Heritage Museum, 2002, on Drohobych.

Avituv, Avraham Yitzhak (Birenboim). *From My Father's House: Memories of Childhood in my Birth Town Husiatyn.* Tel Aviv: Self-published, 1965.

Drix, Samuel. *Witness to Annihilation—Surviving the Holocaust: A Memoir.* Washington, D.C.: Brassey's, 1994, on L'viv.

Fremont, Helen. *After Long Silence: A Memoir.* New York: Random House, 1999, on Buchach and L'viv.

Halpern, Mordechai. *A Family and a City: In Prosperity and in Ruin.* Tel Aviv: Traklin, 2003, in Hebrew, on Buchach.

Halpern, Sam. *Darkness and Hope.* New York: Shengold Books, 1997, on Khorostkov (Khorostkiv) near Husiatyn.

Herzog, Pesach. *In the Shadow of the Black Eagle: Memories of Tarnopol in 1939–1945.* Tel Aviv: Yaron Golan, 1996, in Hebrew.

Horowitz, Irene and Carl. *Of Human Agony.* New York: Shengol Publishers, 1992, on L'viv and Boryslav (Boryslaw).

Kahane, David. *Lvov Ghetto Diary.* Trans. Jerzy Michalowicz. Amherst: University of Massachusetts Press, 1990.

Katz, Etunia Bauer. *Our Tomorrows Never Came.* New York: Fordham University Press, 2000, on Buchach.

Karl, Mali. *Escape a la Vida.* Lima: Imprenta Charito E.I.R.L., 1989, on Buchach.

Lewin, Kurt I. *Przeżyłem: Saga świętego Jura spisana w roku 1946.* Warsaw: Zeszyty Literackie, 2006, on L'viv.

———. *A Journey through Illusions.* Santa Barbara: Fithian Press, 1994, on L'viv.

Milch, Baruch. *And the Heaven May Be Void.* Trans. and ed. Shosh Milch-Avigail and Ephraim F. Stern. Jerusalem: Yad Vashem, 1999, in Hebrew; Polish edition: *Baruch Milch, Testament* [original title: *Szkodliwe robactwo ludzkości, czyli mój testament po Hitlerjadzie*]. Warsaw: Ośrodek KARTA, 2001, on Podhajce (Pidhaitsi) and Tłuste (Tovste).

Rosenberg, Blanca. *To Tell at Last: Survival under False Identity, 1941–45.* Urbana: University of Illinois Press, 1993, on Kolomyia.

Rosner, Mina. *I Am a Witness.* Winnipeg: Hyperion Press, 1990, on Buchach.

Soltan, Christina. *Under Strange Skies.* London: Melville Press, 1948, includes account of Buchach under Soviet occupation.

Wells, Leon Weliczker. *The Janowska Road.* New York: Macmillan, 1963, on L'viv.

Yones, Eliyahu. *At the Edge of the Pit*. Jerusalem: Yad Vashem, 1960, in Hebrew; German translation, *Die Straße nach Lemberg: Zwangsarbeit und Widerstand in Ostgalizien 1941–1944*. Frankfurt am Main: Fischer Taschenbuch Verlag, 1999, on L'viv.

———. *Smoke in the Sand: The Jews of Lwów during the War 1939–1944*. Jerusalem: Yad Vashem, 2001, in Hebrew.

Zaderecki, Tadeusz. *When the Swastika Ruled in Lwów: The Destruction of the Jewish Community through the Eyes of a Polish Writer*. Trans. Zvi Arad. Jerusalem: Yad Vashem, 1982, in Hebrew.

Memoir and Travel Literature

Baselgia, Guido, and Verena Dohrn. *Galizien*. Frankfurt am Main: Jüdischer Verlag, 1993.

Döblin, Alfred. *Journey to Poland*. Trans. Joachim Neugroschel. 1925; New York: Paragon House Publishers, 1991.

Dohrn, Verena. *Reise nach Galizien: Grenzlandschaften des alten Europa*. Berlin: Philo, 2000.

Landmann, Salcia. *Erinnerungen an Galizien*. Munich: Knaur, 1983.

Morgenstern, Soma. *In einer anderen Zeit: Jugendjahre in Ostgalizien*. Berlin: Aufbau Taschenbuch Verlag, 1999.

Pollack, Martin. *Galizien: Eine Reise durch die verschwundene Welt Ostgaliziens und der Bukowina*. Frankfurt am Main: Insel Verlag, 2001.

Schieb, Roswitha. *Reise nach Schlesien und Galizien: Eine Archäologie des Gefühls*. Berlin: Berlin Verlag, 2000.

Simonek, Stefan, and Alois Woldan, eds. *Europa Erlesen: Galizien*. Klagenfurt: Wieser Verlag, 1998.

ABOUT THE AUTHOR

OMER BARTOV is the John P. Birkelund Distinguished Professor of European History at Brown University. He is the author of, among other books, *The "Jew" in Cinema* (Indiana), *Germany's War and the Holocaust* (Cornell), *Mirrors of Destruction* (Oxford), *Murder in Our Midst* (Oxford), and *Hitler's Army* (Oxford).

INDEX OF NAMES

INDEX OF PLACE-NAMES

Milton Keynes UK
Ingram Content Group UK Ltd.
UKHW010607010923
427853UK00004B/31/J

9 780691 131214